CW01261866

The British Natural History Collection

Volume 5

POLECATS

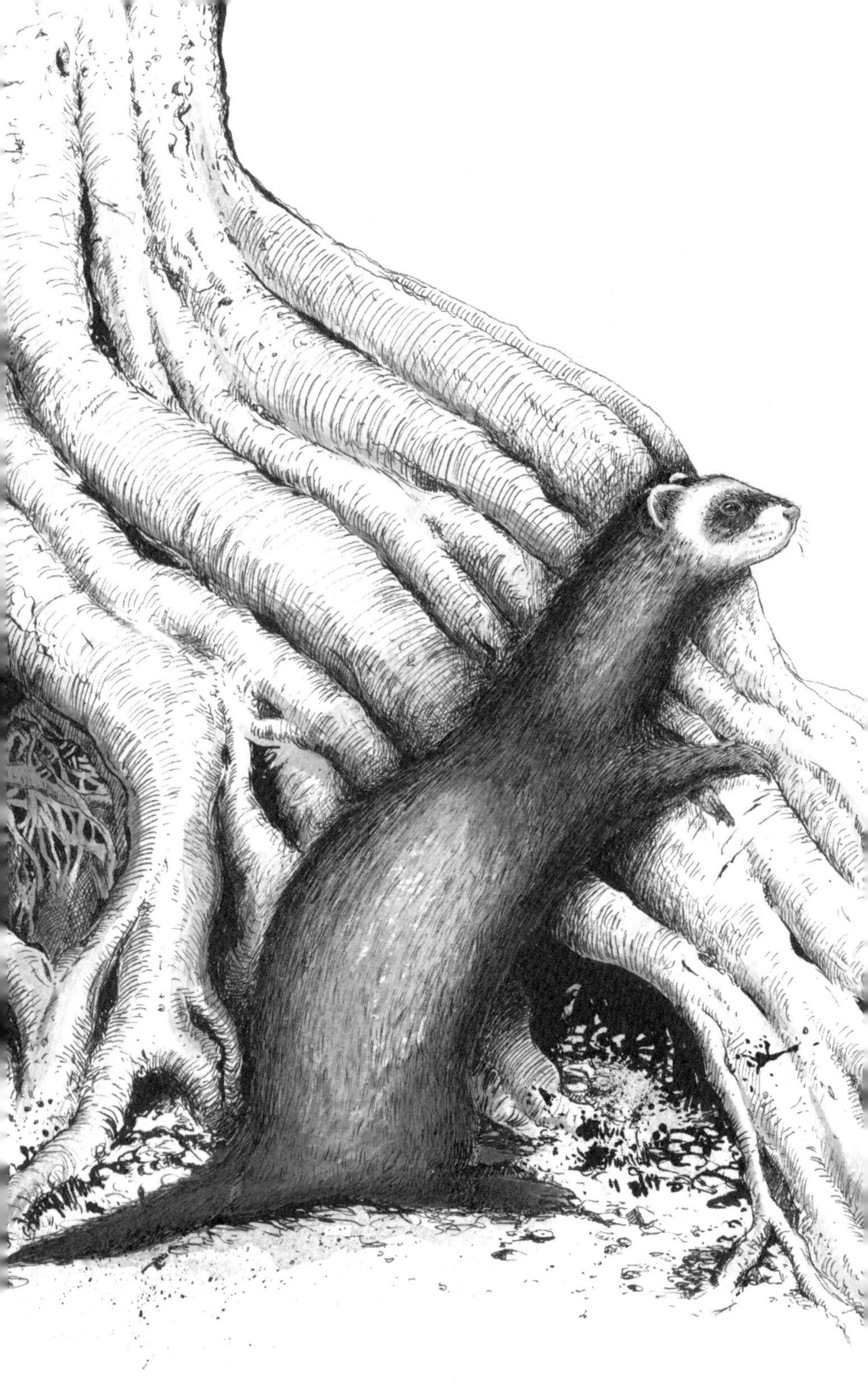

POLECATS

Johnny Birks

Illustrations by Antony Griffiths
Photographs by Richard Bowler

Whittet Books

Whittet Books Ltd
1 St John's Lane
Stansted
Essex CM24 8JU
mail@whittetbooks.com
www.whittetbooks.com

First published 2015

Text © Johnny Birks 2015
Illustrations and Polecat painting © Antony Griffiths 2015
Photographs © Richard Bowler 2015

This publication is in copyright. Subject to statutory exception and to the provisions of relevant collective licensing agreements, no part of this publication may be reproduced, transmitted or stored in a retrieval system, in any form or by any means, without the prior permission of Whittet Books Ltd.

Whittet Books Ltd has no responsibility for the persistence or accuracy of URLs for external or third party internet websites referred to in this publication, and does not guarantee that any content on such websites is, or will remain, accurate or appropriate.

A catalogue record for this publication is available from the British Library.

ISBN 978 1 873580 98 1

Designed by Lodge Graphics

CONTENTS

Acknowledgements	1
Preface	3
What is a polecat?	5
Polecats of the world	6
Origins, relations and hybridisation	8
Time to get to know our polecat	10
A confusing mixture of polecats and ferrets	12
Ferret origins and domestication	13
Separating true polecats from ferrety ones	19
A stinker of a reputation	24
How we nearly lost the polecat from Britain	31
Decline and fall	31
The beginnings of recovery in Wales	36
Recolonisation of England	39
Polecats in Scotland?	41
The role of reintroductions	42
Current distribution and future spread	45
The polecat's status in Europe	47
Size, shape and colour	48
Size and shape	48
Skeletal stuff	51
Colouration	52
Quantifying colour variations in polecats	54
Rare colour morphs	56
Fighting and mating scars – the white tufts of passion!	57
Polecat senses	58
How many polecats?	60
Social life	64
Territoriality	64
Communication	65
The polecat's social calendar	67
Mating and pregnancy	69
Birth and juvenile development	74
Juvenile dispersal	77
Lifespan	78
Trophic matters (food and foraging)	79
Scats tell all	79
Foraging for rabbits – underground operations	83
Gender variations in diet	84
Rat control	86
A modern dietary generalist	87
Pre-historic anuran specialism?	89
Polecat habitats	96
Broad habitat selection	96
Habitat preferences on lowland farmland	97
Microhabitat selection	98
Suburban and 'garden decking' polecats	99
Work, rest and play	102
Dens	102
Activity patterns	105
Relations with other carnivores	106
Self-defence	110
Sick bay or health matters	112
Parasites	112
Diseases and other ailments	112
Causes of injury and death	115
Polecats and roads – a love-hate relationship?	115
Secondary rodenticide poisoning	119
Traps	120
Studying polecats	122
Field signs – a matter of scats and tracks	122
Can we separate polecat and mink footprints?	124
Camera-trapping	128
Live-trapping	130
Hair tubes and footprint tunnels	131
Watching polecats	131
Polecats and the law	133
Further reading	134
Sources of Information	135
Index	136

The photographs are between pages 58 and 59.

ACKNOWLEDGEMENTS

The polecat has not been an easy animal to get to know, and many people have helped me along the way. I was first led down the mustelid path by my darling, eccentric aunt Molly who got me hooked on the weasel family by giving me Pico, my first ferret. My parents (who blamed Molly for much of my odd behaviour subsequently) generously supported me through the 'ferret years' – for Pico was the first of many – and into a stuttering mammal research career. At Exeter University Ian Linn guided me through a PhD on feral mink. Paul Chanin and Don Jefferies became my mustelid gurus in whose footsteps I still tread, with Paddy Sleeman my wild Irish mustelid mentor. The late Vincent Weir gave me my big break when he employed me to study polecats with The Vincent Wildlife Trust (VWT), a special, quirky organisation that for 40 years has done great things for Britain's less charismatic mammals. For their inspiration and guidance I acknowledge two other great men who are no longer with us: Ken Walton, pioneer polecat researcher, and Russell Coope, passionate champion of Britain's wild predators.

The VWT took me on in 1993, and so began my long involvement with the charming but little-loved polecat. Long-term studies are precious because they yield greater insights than the usual three-year funding term, and the VWT has that rare staying power; the only downside is that, more than 20 years later, I am still known locally as 'the polecat man'. Despite the enduring nickname, I am grateful to all landowners who tolerated my nocturnal loitering in search of polecat facts. The VWT still does great work on polecats and I am indebted to Lizzie Croose for keeping me informed of new research findings.

Much of what I have learnt about polecats, and consequently much that fills this book, has been selflessly offered as records and observations by countless naturalists, researchers, VWT colleagues and members of The Mammal Society. Too many to thank by name (though some are mentioned in the text), they are part of the great wildlife-mad community that makes Britain so special; just how special was revealed by an envious Iberian friend who once told me, 'We could never do such surveys in my country – nobody would bother to stop to look at road casualty polecats, let alone collect and deliver them to us!' So I thank all those who have contributed to the VWT's polecat surveys over the years and have added in other ways to the sum of polecat knowledge. I am also grateful to the foreign mammalogists, notably Andrzej Zalewski, Vadim Sidorovich, Sim Broekhuizen, Thierry Lodé, Margarida Santos-Reis and Darius Weber, who have stretched the horizons of my polecat knowledge through their studies across the water. And I thank James McKay for his ferrety wisdom.

Within the army of people who have helped me I salute four wise generals in their role as key collaborators: Andrew Kitchener of the National Museums Scotland masterminded curation of the huge collection of polecat carcasses gathered by the VWT and its foot soldiers, developed a pelage scoring system for separating pure polecats from 'ferrety' hybrids and organised a series of student projects that produced valuable new information, notably about the polecat's diet in England; Richard Shore of the Centre for Ecology and Hydrology led us down his toxic path to enlightenment on the impact of rodenticides on polecats; and geneticists Angus Davison (University of Nottingham) and Mafalda Costa (University of Cardiff) shed crucial light on the tangled relationship between polecats and ferrets in Britain.

In spite of this wealth of information I sometimes struggled to produce any text from one month to the next, so I warmly thank the supremely tolerant Shirley Greenall, publisher at Whittet Books, for patiently guiding this project from start to finish. A more ancient spirit (pre-Cambrian actually) played its part when the words ran dry: crepuscular walks on the Malvern Hills with Beaver and Dooley were a frequent source of perspective on life, polecats and everything. Once scruffily complete, my friends Lizzie Croose and John Martin kindly read through a draft and offered many helpful comments.

Finally, I owe huge thanks to Helen for choosing to share her life with a mustelid obsessive. Who else would have calmly tolerated the nights disturbed by radio-tracking, the eternally stinking family car, and surprises (both furry and faecal) lurking in the freezer, as if these were all normal? Her support has been awesome.

This book is dedicated to our granddaughters Melissa and Kaitlyn.

PREFACE

It feels as if the polecat is giving us Britons a second chance: our ancestors despised it more than any other animal and persecuted it to the very brink of extinction. At the height (or depth?) of our onslaught in the early 1900s it survived in its small Cambrian refuge and has since spread back to test our tolerance again. Just as civilizations are judged by how they treat their minorities, how will we shape up this time? So far so good it seems, for the story is a positive one and we have much to cheer about, polecat-wise. Our attitude to nature matured through the last century so that now we can value wild animals in ways beyond how tasty or troublesome they might be. So today we can enjoy our brief encounters with polecats, or at least draw pleasure from knowing that they are back in our parish. When so many other species are in decline in Britain, it has been a treat for me to be involved in studying the recovery of one that bucks that trend.

The polecat's recovery in Britain is one of the least celebrated wildlife success stories of recent times, probably because it has done it discreetly and all by itself with no active human involvement. Whilst our spirits have been lifted by the more obvious return of cronking ravens and mewing buzzards, and by the carefully managed reintroductions of red kites and sea eagles, the unfamiliar, nocturnal polecat has slipped back under the radar. This unobtrusiveness makes it all the more magical: a secret touch of ancient wildness returning uninvited is good for the soul in our over-managed world; the polecat brings hidden spice to our bland modern landscapes; and it is part of a subtle re-wilding of Britain that, piece by piece, might rebuild ecosystems fractured by intensive agriculture and impoverished by historical persecution of their more troublesome inhabitants. Whether we appreciate it or not, our lives are richer for the polecat's return. So let's view it and our new-found tolerance as symbols of hope that we might, one day, live in greater harmony with the natural world that sustains us in both body and mind.

Restoring long-lost predators to their rightful place in modern ecosystems is often controversial: we love and admire them while they are rare and confined to tracts of rugged wilderness, then tolerance fades in some quarters when their numbers increase and they dare to live close to humans once more. So the resurgent polecat will present us with some challenges, especially for keepers of game and poultry who may need help adapting their husbandry to cope with a world in which predators must be allowed to thrive. Nor is the polecat the only ancient *disparu* returning to test us modern Brits once again; the graceful pine marten is on a similar journey in Scotland where, regrettably, its recovery is not welcomed by all.

Excitingly, there is still a lot to learn about polecats as they repopulate Britain and elbow their way back into the guild of carnivores from which we ripped them more than a hundred years ago. Learning about polecats is no longer the preserve of academics: throughout Britain there are bands of highly skilled so-called 'amateur' naturalists and members of local Mammal Groups using modern techniques, such as camera traps, to make valuable observations of polecat behaviour. Anyone and everyone can join in the fun of re-acquainting ourselves with one of Britain's least-known mammals.

WHAT IS A POLECAT?

In Britain ours is the European or western polecat *Mustela putorius*, which, as its English name implies, is mainly found in Western and central Europe. The English name unhelpfully suggests some cat-like allegiance, but polecats, with their five-toed prints and impressively smelly, rear-end defensive armoury, most definitely belong to the Mustelinae, the weasel sub-family of the Mustelidae. Our polecat is one of six mustelids native to Great Britain: the others being the Eurasian otter, badger, pine marten, stoat and weasel; the American mink (which is surprisingly similar to the polecat in appearance and behaviour, though not very closely related) is Britain's only wild 'alien' mustelid following its escape from fur farms in the mid twentieth century. Like the weasel, the polecat isn't found in Ireland, probably because it didn't nip across the land bridge in time before the Irish Sea formed after the last Ice Age.

There are other species of polecat that share common characteristics with ours: they are all terrestrial hunters with short legs and long, fairly slim, sinuous bodies and short to medium-length tails – this shape suits their habit of exploring holes and burrows in search of prey; within the mustelid family polecats are medium-sized, with body lengths 40–80 cm and weights 0.7–2.2 kg (so they are bigger than stoats and weasels, but smaller than badgers and otters); they are sexually dimorphic, meaning that within each species the males are bigger than the females; they live mainly nocturnal and solitary lives, with each individual defending a separate territory, and there is little interaction between adults except during the mating season; although polecats have short legs, so spend most of their lives close to (or beneath) the ground, they like to stand up on their hind legs to get a better view (or scent) of their surroundings; and finally, when threatened, polecats emit a powerful stink from their anal scent glands to deter potential predators, and they advertise this defence via bold aposematic (warning) colouring in their fur; so polecats tend to have striking markings, especially on their faces where the light and dark banding resembles a bandit's mask in some species. Such advertising is not uncommon in the animal kingdom (usually black or dark brown combined with white, cream or yellow), and serves to warn aggressors of an impressive bite, sting, poison, stink or other nastiness; other examples are the badger (bite), skunk (stink), fire salamander (poison), wasps (sting) and certain football teams...

Polecats of the world

There is a small band of similar polecat species spread around the world, mostly in the milder parts of the northern hemisphere (polecats are not adapted to survive in the cold Polar Regions). The western polecat's range extends from southern Scandinavia southward to the Mediterranean and Black Seas, and from the Atlantic coast of Iberia eastward to the Ural Mountains in western Russia; it is absent from Ireland and parts of southeastern Europe, such as the Adriatic coast of the Balkans and most of Greece. In the twentieth century in the north-eastern parts of its range the western polecat extended its distribution northwards into Karelia and southern Finland, perhaps in response to changes in habitat or climate.

In parts of central and eastern Europe our western polecat's range overlaps with that of the closely related eastern or steppe polecat *Mustela eversmannii*, which is found across the steppes and semi-deserts of Central Asia through Mongolia to China; here it preys mainly upon

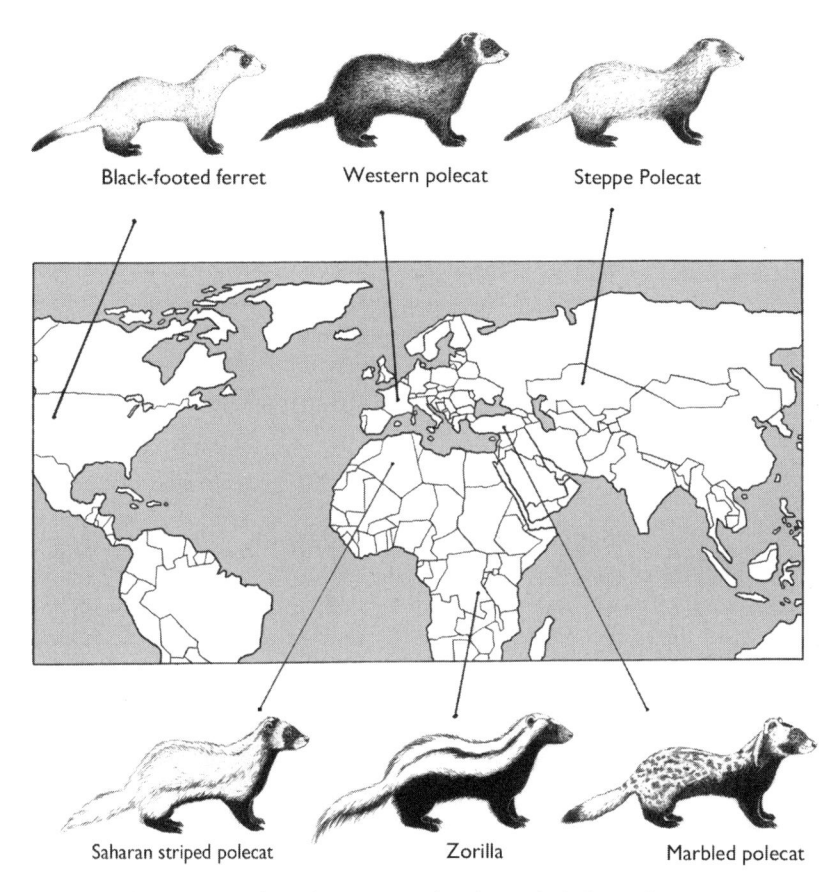

*The western polecat has some strikingly marked close relatives in
North America, Eurasia and Africa.*

steppe rodents such as pikas, hamsters and marmots. Slightly longer than our western polecat, the steppe polecat has a similar dark bandit mask but a paler, shorter-furred, ginger-brown coat with darker brown underparts, legs and tail tip.

In North America, the rare black-footed ferret *Mustela nigripes* (sometimes called the American polecat) is a close relative of both the steppe and western polecats. This long, slim, short-furred polecat looks very much like the steppe polecat, though is generally paler on the body and has even shorter fur and more prominent ears. It is a specialist predator of prairie dogs (social, burrowing rodents), so its historical range in the western prairies of North America correlates closely with that of its prey. Following a massive twentieth-century decline the species was declared extinct in 1979, until a small population was unexpectedly discovered in Wyoming in 1981. Since then, captive breeding and reintroduction efforts have restored self-sustaining populations to several states, but its conservation status remains precarious. The International Union for the Conservation of Nature (IUCN) classes the black-footed ferret as globally endangered.

The little known marbled polecat *Vormela peregusna* (also known as the tiger polecat) has an overlapping but slightly more southerly distribution than the steppe polecat, from south-eastern Europe (Serbia, Montenegro, Macedonia, southern Romania, Bulgaria, Turkish Thrace and north-eastern Greece) through Libya, Syria, Jordan, Palestine, Afghanistan, Iran, the Ukraine, and Russia to western China. This is the smallest of the polecats and the most strikingly marked: on a mainly black background it has bold white facial markings similar to the western polecat's bandit mask, but with more prominent, white-tipped ears; the fur on its body has the curious brown and yellow marbled effect that inspired its name; and its brown and yellow tail has a frosting effect due to the white hair tips. Because of its recent population decline, the marbled polecat is listed as vulnerable on the IUCN's Red List of Threatened Species.

Africa has two strikingly marked polecats: the zorilla *Ictonyx striatus* (also called the striped or African polecat) is found throughout the drier, savannah landscapes of sub-Saharan Africa, where it relies upon skunk-like black and white markings to warn potential predators of its foul-smelling defensive armoury; further north is found the similar and closely related Saharan striped polecat *Ictonyx libyca*, which inhabits sparsely vegetated desert fringes, oases and mountains in and around the Sahara desert.

Origins, relations and hybridisation

For years taxonomists have bickered politely about the origins of and relations between the western polecat, steppe polecat and black-footed ferret. All three are thought to have evolved from a common polecat ancestor, *Mustela stromeri*, which arose during the late Villafranchian period one or two million years ago. Modern genetic techniques, and especially the construction of phylogenetic trees based upon quantifiable genetic similarities and differences between species, have recently helped to unravel patterns of relatedness among these and other mustelids; they also suggest likely divergence times (the estimated period during evolutionary history when one particular species separated from another), though these do vary depending upon which technique is applied. For example, the steppe and western polecats, which are confirmed as being very closely related, are believed to have separated either 1.5 million years ago using nucleotide sequences or 0.43 million years ago based upon analyses of mitochondrial cytochrome b genes. This relatively recent separation is further supported by reports that the two species do hybridise to produce fertile offspring in those parts of Eastern Europe where they co-occur.

Whilst we are fairly clear about our polecat's origins in Europe, a whiff of mystery surrounds the status of polecat-like animals in restricted parts of North Africa. For many years wild polecats or polecat-ferrets (typically, and perhaps wrongly, labelled *Mustela putorius furo*) have been reported to occur in the wooded and mountainous Rif area of northern Morocco, and more recently from further east in the Maamoura region of Algeria (where photographs supplied in an article by Mourad Ahmim clearly show a ferret-like animal). The occurrence in North Africa of other mainly Eurasian mammals such as red deer, garden dormouse and wild boar in this Maghrebian Region of the Palearctic means we should not rush to rule out the natural occurrence of some form of the western polecat there; nor can we dismiss historical human interference by the transport of domestic ferrets across the Mediterranean. Because evidence of the animals in Morocco now is very sparse there is an urgent need to apply molecular genetic techniques in order to establish their origins and inform conservation decisions. Adding to the intrigue is the disputed suggestion that North Africa is the location where polecats were first domesticated to create the ferret some two thousand years ago.

The western polecat probably colonised Britain towards the end of the last glaciation, having survived in an ice-free refuge somewhere in southern Europe alongside other members of our modern mammal fauna. Intriguingly, the fossil record in the Late Glacial period revealed evidence of a 'giant polecat' from cave deposits in Kent and Derbyshire, which had a skull some 12 per cent bigger than that of our polecat today. Originally recognised in Germany as a separate species, *Mustela robusta*, this was probably just a larger form of *Mustela putorius* adapted to tackling larger sub-arctic prey such as sousliks (ground squirrels). Despite a presence on mainland Britain as the ice retreated, like some other mammals the polecat apparently never made it across to Ireland.

The third member of our northern polecat gang, the black-footed ferret, probably evolved from the steppe polecat when that species crossed the Bering land bridge from Siberia into North America nearly a million years ago; certainly these two appear so similar that they were regarded as conspecific (part of the same species) in the past. In fact all three 'northern polecats' are so closely related it has even been suggested that they could be viewed as a single circumpolar species shrouding the northern hemisphere like a great, whiffy polecat cloak. But modern genetic techniques now confirm that they are three distinct species, albeit so closely related that they are capable of hybridisation.

Genetic evidence indicates that the next-closest relatives of our three 'circumpolar' polecats are the European mink *Mustela lutreola*, the kolinsky or Siberian weasel *Mustela sibirica* and the Japanese weasel *Mustela itatsi*. Again this is supported by evidence of hybridisation between the western polecat and the European mink in Eastern Europe, a process which, among other pressures, is viewed as a threat to the conservation of the endangered European mink. The American mink *Neovison vison* was once believed to be part of the *Mustela* genus (it was called *Mustela vison* until 2005); but modern genetic techniques confirm that it is a more distant relative, so there is little prospect of hybridisation between our western polecat and the American mink in the many places, such as Britain, where they co-occur.

Time to get to know our polecat

The western polecat (hereafter called 'the polecat' in this book unless avoidance of ambiguity demands otherwise) is one of Britain's least familiar wild mammals, and there are several reasons for this: polecats have been scarce or absent over much of Britain for a long time, surviving mainly in the more sparsely populated west, so most of us have had no chance to encounter one (many people confuse the polecat with the pine marten, a similar and related animal that is equally scarce in Britain, but now recovering in Scotland); polecats are nocturnal so are rarely seen even where they do occur; unlike many mammals such as the badger and otter, polecats don't feature prominently in popular literature, nor does their image appear on tea towels, calendars and place mats (regrettably their potential role in television advertising has been usurped by gangs of meerkats with Russian accents) – one exception is a Heath Robinson drawing entitled *Trapping the Polecat in the Catskill Mountains;* and finally, the polecat has a domesticated relative, the ferret, with which it can cross-breed to produce 'polecat-ferrets' that confuse our perceptions of the true polecat.

A startling example of just how little we know the polecat today took me unawares when I was setting up my field study for The Vincent Wildlife Trust in the early 1990s. I spent a week knocking on farmhouse doors to seek permission for my study in a quiet part of rural east Herefordshire near where I live, an area recolonised by polecats some thirty years earlier so the species was bound to be present and well established. As each door opened I delivered a well-prepared spiel about my survey of polecats with what I hoped was a winning blend of charm and enthusiasm, only to be met in some cases by frowns, shaking heads and more or less polite 'no thank yous'. Perplexed by this unexpected negativity, I changed tack and revisited with a fine photograph of a polecat on clear display; this did the trick and I was welcomed by all landowners in my study area, although most confessed that they had not seen the animal on their land; mink yes, but polecats no.

One farmer apologised for closing the door on me earlier in the week: 'We thought you were something to do with the Poll Tax' (a deeply unpopular version of local rates introduced by the Westminster Government at the time); so not only were most farmers unaware of polecats on their land, but the animal's name was so unfamiliar that it was confused with a similar-sounding hated fiscal measure; and I learnt a lesson about the importance of clear diction and supporting images! When I started live-trapping polecats in 1993 (after my licence was granted by English Nature – the government agency I had earlier worked for), I took the trouble to show them to local farmers and landowners, usually giving them their first clear view of a wild animal that had lived on their land for many years.

A CONFUSING MIXTURE OF POLECATS AND FERRETS

The ferret is a domesticated form of polecat that is kept in captivity either as a working animal (for bolting rabbits and rats), a pet or both. Historically, the ferret was typically a true albino with whitish-yellow fur and pink eyes, but today many ferret-keepers prefer the dark-eyed forms with a variety of fur colours that range from a 'dark-eyed white' (DEW for short) through pale sandy brown to very dark, polecat-like pelage known as fitch or fitchet (old English names for the polecat). Ferret-breeders use evocative names such as sable, panda, champagne, butterscotch and cinnamon to describe the different colours that occur between the albino and the true polecat. Essentially there are five main colour categories recognised by the ferret-keeping fraternity: fitch, albino, silver, sandy and dark-eyed-white.

Interestingly, the occurrence of a range of colour varieties in domestic and feral ferret populations indicates that the genes controlling fur colour are not confined, as one might expect, to a simple split between the recessive gene for albinism and the dominant gene for the standard dark polecat colour; other genes must be involved, as James McKay explains in his *Complete Guide to Ferrets*.

To create and maintain the variety of colours in domestic ferrets, from time to time people have deliberately 'back-crossed' their ferrets with wild polecats. Also, because lost or escaped ferrets have been breeding with wild polecats in Britain for hundreds of years, their genes are well mixed so that a range of 'ferrety' forms now occurs in the wild; some of these look very much like true polecats, with just a few subtle hints of ferret in their colouration. Elsewhere in Britain, where true polecats are either naturally absent (such as some Scottish islands, where ferrets have been released in the mistaken belief that they would control rabbits) or have been eradicated in the past, self-sustaining populations of feral (meaning 'domestic gone wild') ferrets may survive in the wild.

Consequently in many parts of Britain naturalists and biological recorders struggle to separate true polecats from the ferrety ones, leading to uncertainties about the distribution and status of the two forms in the wild. Also, the centuries of polecat and ferret inter-mixing, in both captive and wild-living populations, raises questions of crucial importance to the conservation and legal protection of the true polecat in Britain: which species of polecat was the ferret originally derived from? What is the outcome of competition between polecats and ferrets in the wild? Is the genetic integrity of our polecats under threat? How can conservation policy minimise any such threat? And can our conservation legislation be made to work when the true polecat has some legal protection but an 'impure' or 'ferrety' animal does not? We are reminded just how urgent it is to answer such questions by the parlous conservation status of the Scottish wildcat in the early 2000s: after a serious nineteenth-century decline caused by habitat loss and persecution, the much-diminished wildcat population faces a new threat from hybridisation with domestic and feral cats; our domestic cats originally came from a North African species of wildcat, so hybridisation is introducing alien genes that now erode the genetic integrity of our precious 'Highland Tiger'.

Ferret origins and domestication

The earliest widely accepted reference to humans using ferrets to catch rabbits dates from the first century AD, so domestication of wild polecats probably occurred in Roman times somewhere in the rabbit's surprisingly restricted native range at the time in Iberia and southern France.

As Juliet Clutton-Brock points out in *A Natural History of Domesticated Mammals*, despite a historical report to the contrary, we can probably rule out North Africa as the location of domestication because neither of the ferret's possible polecat ancestors occurs there, although the jury is still out on the question of the origins of polecat-like animals living wild in the Rif area of northern Morocco.

Whilst pinpointing the location and timing of the ferret's domestication is interesting, establishing the correct identity of the wild ancestral polecat species involved is of far greater importance given the evidence of ferret genes now present in Britain's recovering polecat population. Thankfully modern genetic techniques have helped to confirm that the western polecat is the original ancestor of the ferret, which is not surprising since the other candidate, the steppe polecat, has a range that did not coincide at the time with that of the rabbit, the quarry species that was the main driving force behind ferret domestication.

Nevertheless, uncertainty persisted for most of the twentieth century about whether the ferret was derived from the steppe polecat or our western polecat: as early as 1912 Miller suggested that, because of the occurrence of a similarly narrow post-orbital constriction (a 'waist' behind the eye sockets) in the skulls of both the steppe polecat and the domestic ferret, one could not rule out the former as the wild ancestor; in 1932 Pocock challenged this suggestion by showing that the shape and position of the post-orbital constriction were different in the steppe polecat and ferret, leaving the western polecat as the only likely ancestor; subsequently further cranial comparisons by other authors supported this view, also affirming that the steppe polecat's nasal bones differ in shape from the others; and in the 1990s Andrew Kitchener concluded that the ferret's narrow post-orbital constriction probably arose as a simple consequence of its easier life in captivity and the associated lesser development of the jaw muscles (he measured the skulls of feral ferrets from Shetland and found that some were identical to those of wild western polecats, with no narrowing of the post-orbital constriction). Finally, genetic analyses by Angus Davison (1998) and Mafalda Costa (2013), both described more fully later, confirm that the ferret must be derived from the western polecat; so the flawed case for the steppe polecat as a possible ferret ancestor is effectively closed.

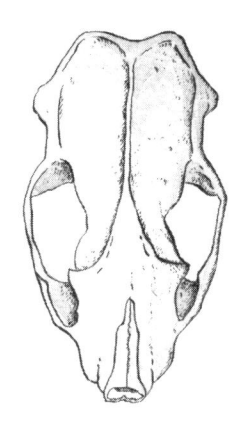

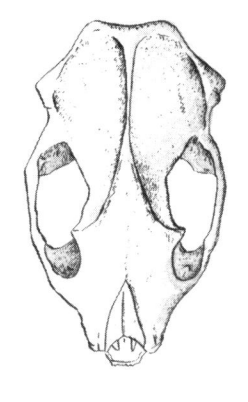

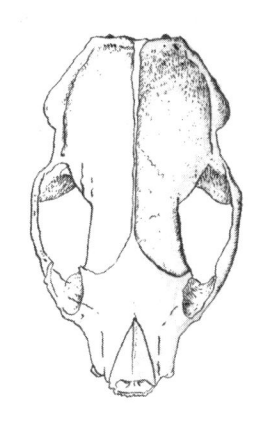

Dorsal views of skulls of steppe polecat (left), domestic ferret (centre) and western polecat (right), showing differences in the shape of the nasal bones and the shape and position of the waist-like post-orbital constriction (redrawn with kind permission of The Vincent Wildlife Trust).

This welcome clarification should help to tidy up the ferret's rather messy taxonomy. Since Linnaeus (rather too hastily?) assigned the ferret to a separate species, *Mustela furo*, in 1758, some authors have instead treated the ferret as either a sub-species or domesticated form of the western polecat (for example using the name *Mustela putorius* f. furo), while others have upheld its questionable status as a discrete species whilst acknowledging its recent polecat ancestry. With the clear evidence about ancestry now available, and knowing that the differences between polecats and ferrets are a consequence of the latter's life in captivity and selective breeding by humans, there is a much stronger case for treating the ferret as simply a domesticated form of the western polecat; but the world of taxonomy moves cautiously, so don't expect an instant change.

How was the polecat domesticated to create the ferret?

It is fun to speculate about the events, thoughts and actions that led to the first western polecat being taken into captivity, somewhere in southern Europe about two thousand years ago, as the precursor to

POLECATS | A CONFUSING MIXTURE OF POLECATS AND FERRETS

the process of domestication that eventually created the ferret. The story that follows below is my best guess at how events may have unfolded, although in reality things may have taken much longer, with many more false turns and mistakes along the way.

Imagine a French or Spanish peasant farmer pausing reflectively at dusk or dawn on the edge of his smallholding, witnessing by chance the effects of a wild polecat hunting within a set of rabbit burrows: he hears the sound of bunny hind feet drumming underground to warn others of an approaching predator; then he sees several rabbits bolting fast from burrows and away, followed occasionally by the questing, bandit-masked face of the polecat appearing briefly at a burrow entrance before turning to continue hunting inside the warren; then finally he hears bumping and squealing as one less fortunate rabbit is caught underground, overpowered and killed by the classic mustelid bite to the neck.

Eager to enrich his family's diet with wild meat, our peasant farmer might think twice the next time he encounters a wild adult polecat in a trap or finds a helpless, orphaned kit. Recalling the bolting rabbits and thinking laterally, he considers how he might engineer that situation to his own convenience in future. Too fierce and smelly to be handled safely, the trapped adult polecat is soon dismissed as useless and killed as usual, but a kit is taken home and given to his children to play with. Ridiculed by his neighbours for taking in and rearing such a despised pest, our thoughtful peasant is spurred on to pursue his 'foolish idea' just so that he can have the last laugh. Because the polecat was very young when taken in, was reared on its own and was handled every day by the children, it grows up relaxed in human company and can be handled safely as an adult; its diet is poor so it is weak and small compared with a wild polecat, but it still enjoys the scent of rabbit!

That autumn, the peasant takes his tame polecat to the rabbit burrows that earlier inspired his project; quietly he places nets over all the burrow entrances and then releases his secret weapon into the most windward one (so that its scent precedes it through the tunnels); deep drumming is swiftly followed by the 'whoosh' into the nets of two fine rabbits, to one of which the polecat is firmly attached by its canine teeth embedded in a bunny bottom. Our peasant is so thrilled by this instant success that he forgives his over-excited polecat for the nasty bite it gave him when he tried to separate it from the rabbit. Carefully concealing his lacerated fingers, he boastfully shows off the dead rabbits and explains how he caught them to his incredulous neighbours. Later that evening, while his family feasts on spit-roast rabbit (and the polecat enjoys warm rabbit guts in its hutch outside), the peasant wonders how in future he can reduce the risk of the polecat getting its teeth into the rabbit underground (and into his own fingers). He knows he is fortunate that his polecat was not strong enough to kill the rabbit underground; had that happened he would either have had a long wait to retrieve it after it had eaten its fill, or he would have had to dig it out.

And so our peasant plans to breed more docile polecats that are less likely to catch and kill the quarry underground, yet are still sufficiently interested in rabbits to enter their burrows willingly so as to bolt them into the nets. With his family's help he hand-rears another wild polecat kit of the opposite sex and, when mature the following spring, mates it with his first one. In every litter over successive generations he monitors the kits' behaviour and kills off all those that show vigour and aggression, always selecting the slowest, weakest, most docile animals for breeding. One summer, much to his amazement, an albino male kit is born in a litter containing four normal-coloured polecats.

This curious, pink-eyed, white-coated animal is more easily tamed than its siblings and easier to spot out in the countryside when later he takes it to catch rabbits, so our incipient ferret-breeder uses this one to sire as many kits as possible. Because the albino coat colour is controlled by a recessive gene, it takes a couple of years of fortuitous back-crossing (Gregor Mendel didn't enlighten us about the genetics of inheritance until the late nineteenth century) before he produces another albino kit to favour in his breeding programme. And so the ferret was launched on the world, perhaps!

As well as being more visible when out ferreting, the albino or pale varieties were probably favoured by early ferret breeders simply because they looked so different from wild polecats, which were heavily persecuted as noxious pests; so perhaps this colour-coding was an essential means of reducing the risk of a valuable animal being clobbered to death as if it were an undesirable polecat; also because dogs are often used in ferreting, a pale ferret is less likely to be mistakenly killed as a rabbit or rat. As well as favouring certain colours, the constant selection of animals that were less likely to kill their quarry and bite their human handlers served to create domestic ferrets that were behaviourally different from wild polecats, typically slower, less vigorous and more docile: as predators they were deliberately hamstrung by this 'unnatural selection' to meet a particular human need, leaving them as rather poor survivors and competitors if they ever found themselves back in the wild.

Separating true polecats from ferrety ones

There are reasons why it is useful to recognise the differences, if we can, between true polecats and 'ferrety hybrids' occurring in the wild in Britain: currently, modest legal protection (against certain methods of killing and taking) applies only to the former; also, naturalists and biological recorders wish to have confidence in the records they make and receive, especially in areas where the polecat has newly re-appeared; and conservation concerns about interactions in the wild between the two forms can only be answered on the basis of clear identification of each. During the 1990s The Vincent Wildlife Trust, guided by Andrew Kitchener of National Museums Scotland (NMS), developed a simple system for separating true polecats from ferrety ones on the basis of pelage characters (fur colour), with a scoring system producing a quantified indication of 'polecatty-ness' (see *Quantifying colour variations in polecats*, page 54).

Most of the polecat and ferret specimens used to develop this system were road casualties from which skins were recovered and preserved at the NMS in Edinburgh. Those that had dark pelage with short pale chin patches conforming to the true polecat phenotype were classed as polecats; those that had paler pelage, or dark pelage with certain 'non-polecatty' pale bits such as on the toes, throat and immediately above the rhinarium (the damp, rubbery bit on the end of the muzzle) and/or scattered pale hairs on the hindquarters, were classed as polecat-ferrets. This approach seemed to work well; it appealed to naturalists because they could make their own judgements based on the appearance of the animals they found; then our geneticist friends got involved and things became rather more complicated!

Firstly, Angus Davison at the University of Nottingham extracted mitochondrial DNA from specimens in the same NMS collection from the 1990s: he identified two cytochrome b lineages indicating that two haplotypes (genetic variants) occurred among all the western polecat and ferret specimens recovered from across Britain. The geographical distribution of these haplotypes was quite different: one (called the Welsh Polecat or 'WP' haplotype because it was presumed to originate from the indigenous polecat) was confined to the historical core of the polecat's range in Wales and western central England; the other (called the Ferret or 'F' haplotype because it was presumed to originate from the domestic ferret) was widely distributed among both polecats and ferrets found in parts of Wales, England and Scotland, including some Scottish Islands. So all the specimens found outside the core historical range that looked like true polecats actually had the presumed Ferret haplotype rather than the presumed ancestral WP haplotype found only in the core historical range. This uncomfortable discovery rather undermined the VWT's practical approach to separating polecats and ferrets on the basis of pelage characters. However, on the positive side, it did reveal that the genetic differences between western polecats and ferrets in Britain are minimal, with each haplotype differing by only a single base transition.

Secondly, geneticist Mafalda Costa and her colleagues at Cardiff University applied a more sophisticated molecular approach to the polecat and ferret conundrum based partly on microsatellite markers from nuclear DNA. Microsatellites are highly variable and can detect patterns of hybridisation between wild animals and their domestic relatives. Mafalda analysed a much larger sample (345 specimens) of British polecat and ferret material than was available in the 1990s; this enabled her to draw some valuable conclusions that build upon Angus Davison's findings: she found that 31 per cent of wild specimens showed genetic evidence of 'admixed ancestry' (i.e. their genes were drawn from both polecats and ferrets) and most of these occurred beyond Wales and the English border counties where polecats were genetically the most 'pure'; and the most 'ferrety' polecats, genetically speaking, were found towards the fringes of the polecat's expanding range (most likely involving dispersing male polecats mating with female ferrets, whose offspring then back-crossed with wild polecats) and further afield where polecats have been reintroduced in northern England and Scotland (where, presumably, their low numbers increase the necessity for matings with local feral ferrets). Finally, Mafalda Costa confirmed that in wild polecats the match between phenotype (what an animal looks like) and genotype (the genetic signature indicating its origins) is not good; in other words some animals that look like polecats have a ferret element in their ancestry and vice versa, a mismatch that was earlier suggested by Angus Davison's work.

Encouragingly, Mafalda found no clear evidence in the wild British polecat population of a 'genetic bottleneck' (the loss of genetic diversity typically afflicting populations that decline to low numbers) that might have been expected following its steep nineteenth-century decline and subsequent restriction to a small stronghold in mid Wales. The inconsistent results from her various 'bottleneck tests' suggest that either the polecat's decline was not as severe as currently believed (unlikely, since Ken Walton's recording in the 1960s confirmed with considerable certainty the absence of polecats from most of their original British range at the time), or the long history of cross-breeding with feral ferrets has effectively countered the expected loss of genetic diversity. So in that sense the bumbling feral ferret has inadvertently done our polecat a big genetic favour!

So what does all this mean for naturalists who want to determine whether the animal they have found run over on the road – and for law-abiding gamekeepers who have caught one in a trap – is a true polecat or a ferrety hybrid? And how much does it matter if, after a thousand years of interbreeding, some of our polecats have a bit of ferret in their ancestry? How 'pure' do we want or need our polecats to be? Is the species really degraded in some way because of ancestral dalliances with a domestic form that, we are now certain, was originally derived from our polecat anyway (albeit somewhere in southern Europe) rather than from a separate species as was once suggested?

Purists may argue that the only true polecat is one that has evidence of ferret neither in its appearance (phenotype) nor in its genetic makeup (genotype); but how well does that approach serve the cause of polecat conservation in the modern world? Rather than condemn as 'impure' an unknown proportion of the successfully expanding polecat population in Britain, surely we are wiser to acknowledge that the species is now simply a little more diverse in appearance, as a consequence of human interference, than it would otherwise have been? There are plenty of mammal precedents elsewhere in Europe (the wolf, wild boar, European bison, Przewalski's horse) where an acknowledged history of hybridisation with domestic congeners does not stand in the way of us accepting them today as 'good' species in the wild.

This pragmatic approach offers advantages over the purist one: it is more inclusive in its assessment of individuals in a population, so that slightly 'ferrety' animals bearing valuable polecat genes need not be viewed as a threat (safer now we are confident that the ferret is simply a domesticated form of our polecat); and it should enable naturalists and biological recorders to continue to make judgements based on phenotype without resorting to the expense of a genetic test for every specimen (if such a test exists in a reliable and affordable form, which currently it doesn't). However, for this approach to work well for polecat conservation we still need a robust and accessible system for assessing phenotype so that the most polecat-like animals can be identified easily.

Confidence in pursuing this inclusive approach depends partly on assumptions that the polecat phenotype will continue to be successful and dominant in the inevitable future mixing of the two forms in the wild; in other words we should be very concerned if, over time, the true polecat phenotype becomes rare and more 'ferrety' forms predominate. Thankfully there is good evidence that the polecat is not threatened in the same way that the Scottish wildcat is: firstly we know that the processes of domestication in the two species were rather different, involving our 'unnatural selection' of characteristics that turned the ferret into a blond and bumbling version of the sharp-witted wild polecat, while the domestic cat was allowed to retain its hunting skills as a home-based mouse-catcher; secondly there is evidence from the VWT's polecat distribution surveys that the polecat phenotype is becoming more widespread as the species recolonises its former range and, most encouragingly, ferrety specimens in the wild seem to fare very badly in survival and reproductive terms when compared with true polecats (over the VWT's 2004–2006 distribution survey the ratio of road casualty polecats to polecat-ferrets in spring was 3:1 and in late summer and autumn it was 20:1, suggesting that the polecat's reproductive output and survival was much higher than the polecat-ferret's). Nevertheless, we must keep monitoring patterns of phenotypic change in time and space to reassure ourselves that the trend is in the right direction from the polecat's viewpoint.

Whilst the range of fur colours arising from the cross-breeding of polecats and ferrets is well known, the behavioural differences between the two forms receive less mention; yet it is these that largely explain why ferrets pose so little threat to the genetic integrity of the wild polecat. Andrew Baines, a ferreter friend from South Wales who helped the VWT with a polecat live-trapping study, was struck by the marked differences in behaviour between his own ferrets and the wild polecats he encountered: 'The polecats were so much more alert and agile, so much quicker and stronger, had so much more vigour.' This simple comparative observation reflects the striking impact that domestication has had on the ferret's ability to survive in the wild, especially where true polecats are present to compete with them.

A STINKER OF A REPUTATION

In historical times the polecat in Britain had a truly awful reputation and our ancestors apparently loathed it more than any other mammal. Their vitriol focused mainly on the polecat's defensive stink and its predation of livestock and other pestilential qualities, which are reflected in the huge number of colloquial names with which we have burdened the animal over the years: the old English name foulmart (and the variants *foumat* and *foumard*), leading to the modern Welsh name *ffwlbart*, was used to separate the polecat from the less pungent *sweetmart* or pine marten; the current Latin name *Mustela putorius* translates as 'foul-smelling musk-bearer', with earlier variations being *Putorius putorius* ('stinky stinker'?) and *Putorius foetidus* ('stinky and foul'?); and the modern English name 'polecat' possibly derives from the French *poule-chat* or 'chicken-cat' – a reference to the polecat's reputation as a wicked killer of poultry (although the polecat's modern French name is *putois*, which translates roughly as 'stinker'); alternatively, the *pol* element may have come from the Gaelic word for hole (referring to the animal's dwelling or hunting behaviour) or from the Old English *ful*, meaning foul; or polecat might even come from a truncation of the Latin *Pollutus catus*, yet another smelly reference. The old English names *fitch*, *fitchew*, *fitchou* and *fitchet* probably derive from the Old French *fissel* or *fissau*, meaning nasty or smelly, or even from the French phrase *fétide chat*. In his book *Silent Fields: The long decline of a nation's wildlife*, Roger Lovegrove suggests the polecat had more colloquial names than any other animal in Britain, probably because in the Middle Ages it was very familiar to people and was viewed as a nuisance by most: there were endless regional and local variations, with at least 20 different versions reported in the Bedfordshire/Hertfordshire area, for example.

In his thought-provoking paper *The foulmart: what's in a name?* on the origins of the polecat's Welsh name *ffwlbart*, Welsh language specialist Duncan Brown uses linguistic evidence to wonder whether the polecat really is native to Britain, or whether it could have been introduced at some point: he notes that the polecat is one of three long-established mammals in Wales that does not have a Welsh name of Celtic origin; the other two being the fallow deer and rabbit, both introduced species.

Considering that Celtic British and its daughter language Welsh pre-date modern English, Brown poses the reasonable question as to why a presumed native mammal should have been given a Welsh name derived from the Medieval English *foulmart*, especially when the other native small mustelids all have Welsh names of Celtic origin? Offering evidence both for and against native status, including the possibility that Welsh speakers might have abandoned the polecat's earlier Celtic name in favour of an English one for some reason, Brown suggests that radiocarbon dating of subfossil polecat remains from Britain could resolve the issue.

Unsurprisingly, given the animal's dreadful, foul-smelling image, in the Middle Ages the word polecat (with some variation in spelling) was used as a form of insult or abuse directed towards vagabonds, prostitutes and others of low repute. Even William Shakespeare, in *The Merry Wives of Windsor*, joins the fray with: 'Out of my door you witch! You hag, you baggage, you poulcat, you runnion!' The abusive habit has lingered into modern times, with *Hansard* (the official written record of UK parliamentary debates) recording that on 2 March 1978 Michael Foot, leader of Her Majesty's Opposition at the time, unkindly (to polecats?!) said of cabinet minister Norman Tebbit: 'It is really time for him to try to let the nicer side of his nature emerge. It is not necessary that every time he rises he should give his famous imitation of a semi-house-trained polecat.' This sort of parliamentary insult might have been inspired by the American cartoonist Culver who, in the 1890s, frequently depicted disgraced politicians and other miscreants as trapped polecats; such abuse was repeated by British Members of Parliament at least half a dozen times during the 1980s, culminating in Norman Buchan's (biologically confused) metaphorical contribution on 13 February 1989: 'Indeed, odious and poisonous; like a polecat, he never changes his spots'.

Such abuse of the polecat's name is not confined to Britain: in the Netherlands (where the word for polecat is *bunzing*) Bart Noord tells me that officers in the Dutch navy warn their colleagues after a particularly pungent visit to the toilet by saying, 'I am so sorry chaps, I seem to have released a bunzing in there'; and *tchórz*, the Polish word for polecat, also means 'coward' in that language. In France (where they call the polecat *putois* or 'stinker') I was told an awful racist joke about three men of different nationalities who made a bet that each could share a cave with *un putois* for longer than the others; after two of the men had left early because of the smell, *le putois* ran out screaming that it could no longer tolerate the stink of the third man.

Predictably, the depth of loathing historically directed towards the polecat in Britain is matched by the great intensity of its persecution at the time. Most inedible wild animals, and especially the predatory ones, were regarded as a worthless nuisance in the dark days before the birth of modern nature conservation in the early twentieth century, by which time we had exterminated some and made others extremely rare; but the polecat was clobbered harder than most. In *Silent Fields* Roger Lovegrove explores the patterns of culling in Britain of those animals that we labelled as 'vermin' through analyses of parish and estate records from the sixteenth century onwards. Notably, churchwardens' accounts provide a detailed tally of the bounties paid under the Vermin Act of 1566 for the heads of certain species, and these can be used to compare numbers killed between parishes and over different years. Such comparisons led Lovegrove to conclude: 'Apart from the Fox, no mammal was killed in more parishes in England and Wales between the seventeenth and nineteenth centuries than the unfortunate polecat...Furthermore no other animal (except Mole) was killed in anything approaching its numbers.'

On top of this onslaught the polecat was hunted for sport with hounds in some areas, especially in the north of England. Also polecats were trapped and killed for their skins because their thick winter coat, then known as *fitch*, was of some value to the fur trade (wild polecats were harvested for their fur in other parts of their range, notably in Russia where, reportedly, over half of the global supply of polecat pelts originated before the First World War): a record of the number and price of polecat pelts (called 'Foumart') on sale at the annual Dumfries Fur Market in south-west Scotland indicates up to 600 pelts were on offer per year in the 1820s and 30s, with peak prices of 18 shillings per furrier's dozen while the polecat was common; then the price rose to 36 shillings in the 1860s as the population declined and pelt numbers fell accordingly, with the Dumfries Fur Market record noting comments such as 'getting scarce', 'very scarce', 'becoming rare' and, tellingly in the 1870s, 'no foumart'. Finally, in the late nineteenth century, a growing army of gamekeepers brought a more organised approach to the control and eradication of predators; their impact upon the polecat population of Britain was devastating, as we shall see later.

So why was the polecat so despised and so heavily persecuted when compared with other so-called vermin? The answer lies in some simple fundamentals of polecat biology: Firstly, polecats have always chosen to live close to humans, especially around cottages and farmsteads where commensal rodents and flocks of poultry are tempting prey, and cluttered barns and log piles provide safe daytime resting sites. My radio-tracking study of polecats in the west of England with The Vincent Wildlife Trust (VWT) revealed many examples of wild polecats sleeping by day in sheds, garages and haystacks, then emerging after dusk to forage in farmyards and gardens as the human inhabitants drew their curtains and turned on their televisions. This cohabitation meant that conflicts of interest have always been especially likely between polecats and humans; this was particularly so in the past when many more people lived and worked on the land than do today, typically in rambling rural cottages with a few chickens and ducks and attendant infestations of rats and mice.

Secondly, being a strictly nocturnal predator and perfectly designed for squeezing through small gaps, the polecat can find and exploit any weakness in the poultry-keeper's defences under cover of darkness; this was especially so before the invention of strong wire mesh for protecting penned birds. For this reason the polecat would have been cursed frequently and hated by all keepers of ducks, chickens, game, ornamental fowl and other small livestock.

Thirdly, close encounters with polecats in the past were eye-wateringly unpleasant and consequently memorable: when a polecat is frightened or injured, such as cornered in a hen-house by a cottager or held in a painful 'leg-hold' trap (no longer legal in Britain, though some modern legal spring traps also fail to kill cleanly), it emits a powerful 'defensive stink' from its anal scent glands that is almost unbearable at close quarters; and the striking 'bandit mask' pattern of light and dark fur on the polecat's face helps anyone whose sense of smell has been so assaulted to remember the experience when they next meet the animal.

Today, having eradicated the polecat from much of Britain beyond living memory, we are unaware of how deeply our forebears despised the animal. Considering how awful its image was in the past, perhaps

POLECATS | A STINKER OF A REPUTATION

driving the polecat to the very brink of extinction was, with hindsight, an accidental act of kindness. Its enforced absence from most counties for a hundred years or more has almost wiped the slate clean, giving us

A polecat caught in a gin trap is held alive until the trapper comes to kill it; although legal and intended to kill humanely, some modern spring traps produce the same painful effect.

the opportunity to offer it a more tolerant reception second time around. I say 'almost' because, of course, there are places in the west of Britain where the polecat never disappeared, and echoes of its old reputation linger on. I remember meeting elderly farmers in Herefordshire in the early 1990s who told me things about polecats that, had I believed them, would have made my hair stand on end (bear in mind that I was doing a field study of polecats involving wandering the fields on my own at night, with occasional rests on the ground when a nap was needed): 'they chew the ears off sheep as they lie sleeping in the fields at night' and, more alarmingly: 'they spring up to bite grown men on the back of the neck, causing paralysis and death'.

Thankfully, such bizarre folk tales are exceptions to the general rule: apart from occasional insulting references in *Hansard* and negative quotes like *'to stink like a polecat'*, which was common in my grandparents' day but is no longer heard today, the polecat has effectively dropped out of our popular culture and is unfamiliar to most of us, including many naturalists. Like a commercial product or political party emerging from a period of deep unpopularity, the polecat can be viewed as ripe for rebranding. I hope this book might play some part in that process.

The polecat in modern popular culture

Slowly but surely the polecat's name and image have begun to creep back into our modern culture and consciousness, with several examples of the word 'polecat' used in a positive light that was unthinkable 200 years ago: *The Polecat Inn* is a popular gastropub at Prestwood near Great Missenden in Buckinghamshire, with its pub sign featuring a replica of Archibald Thorburn's 1920 painting of the animal itself; *The Polecats* is a neo-rockabilly band – they chose the name to replace their original one, *Cult Heroes*, because it felt too punk – formed in North London in 1977, with its most successful LP *Polecats Are Go* released by Mercury in 1981; continuing the musical theme, across the pond (where 'polecat' is slang for the skunk) in 2006 the Texan singer Ray Wylie Hubbard released a raunchy country blues song entitled *Polecat* that describes the animal's stimulating effect upon his partner:

My baby took a polecat, swung it around her head
Threw it off in the wood said 'I smell like you now, so let's go to bed'

In 1995 Julia MacRae Books published *Pyne*, a fiction book by Jonathan Guy about a pair of polecats forced to flee their Welsh mountain home and travel to settle in England; in May 2005 *The Pink Lady PoleCats* became the first all-female team to complete The Scott Dunn Polar Challenge, a gruelling 360-mile race to the North Pole.

The polecat has lent its name to a small number of forward-looking British businesses and their goods and services: a neat play on words is a rigging device called the *Polecat* used by lighting engineers; the *Polecat Screen Print* is a small firm based in Cornwall; and the *Polecat Company* is a software and services company formed in 2007 that transforms internet content into strategic insights for executive level decision-making; *Polecat Properties* is a Sussex-based firm specialising in residential lettings and property management. And talking of properties, in England there are at least two Polecat Lanes, one of which, near Horsham, contains a Polecat Cottage; there is a Polecat Road near Braintree; and, near Lewes, there is a whole row of Polecat Cottages.

HOW WE NEARLY LOST THE POLECAT FROM BRITAIN

Decline and fall
Remarkably, despite all the trapping, poisoning and general beastliness that our ancestors did to them throughout the Middle Ages, polecats apparently remained widespread in Britain until the 1800s, although there were some earlier local extinctions: for example, parish records indicate that the polecat was lost from most of Kent during the mid 1700s. However, after the Industrial Revolution poured massive new wealth into the countryside in the 1800s, the anthropogenic pressure upon polecats moved up to a new level: the rise of driven game shooting as a new recreation among the land-owning industrialists provided an extra motive for getting rid of polecats and other predatory mammals and birds. Gamekeepers were employed on sporting estates to protect wild game, to rear and release game birds and to eradicate any predators that might kill the game before the guns did. Using a range of devices and methods (mainly trapping, shooting and poisoning) that are mostly illegal today, or at least deployed much less intensively, they did a very impressive job.

National census data show that the number of gamekeepers employed in Britain peaked at 23,056 in 1911; these can be viewed as the professional tip of a much larger iceberg of rural workers involved in predator removal at that time, with many farmers, shepherds, cottagers and farm labourers involved on a part-time or casual basis. Regional variations in

The thoroughly inhumane gin trap was one of the main ways of catching polecats until its use became illegal in Britain in 1958.

gamekeeper numbers suggest that pressure upon predators was generally greater in the south and east than in the north and west. The impact upon the distribution and status of predators in Britain was striking, with three mammals and three birds – pine marten, polecat, wildcat, red kite, buzzard and hen harrier – showing marked population declines and range contractions partly or wholly caused by intensive predator control linked to game preservation during the late 1800s and early 1900s. Of these the polecat was among the worst affected, with extinctions logged county by county in naturalists' published accounts in the Victorian and Edwardian era.

An analysis of this literature was used to construct a famous paper in the journal *Mammal Review* in 1977 by Langley and Yalden entitled *The decline of the rarer carnivores in Great Britain during the nineteenth century*. They listed the likely extinction periods for the polecat, pine marten and wildcat for each county in mainland Britain and constructed a retrospective series of four distribution maps for each species from 1800 to 1915 to illustrate the pattern of decline. The polecat series is the most dramatic of the three because it suggests the fastest change in status and distribution over this period: unlike the wildcat and pine marten, both of which in some areas were already extinct or had become scare in 1800 due to woodland clearance, the polecat was widespread and common in 1800; but by 1850 it was scarce in the Scottish borders, the East Midlands of England and large parts of southern England; by 1880 polecats were scarce everywhere except in the north-west Highlands of Scotland, north Cumbria and in mid Wales, and were extinct in much of eastern and central-southern Scotland, as well as in the London area and in Essex and Kent; by 1915 the polecat was extinct across the great majority of Britain outside of Wales, with tiny pockets of scarce, remnant presence shown in Sutherland, north Cumbria and a few question marks in the south Pennines and the Welsh Marches.

This staggering contraction in polecat distribution in little over a hundred years had nothing to do with habitat change and everything to do with direct killing linked mainly to game shooting. In his book *Game Heritage* Stephen Tapper acknowledges the connection: 'There seems little doubt that trapping and shooting by gamekeepers were largely responsible for this reduction in range…'

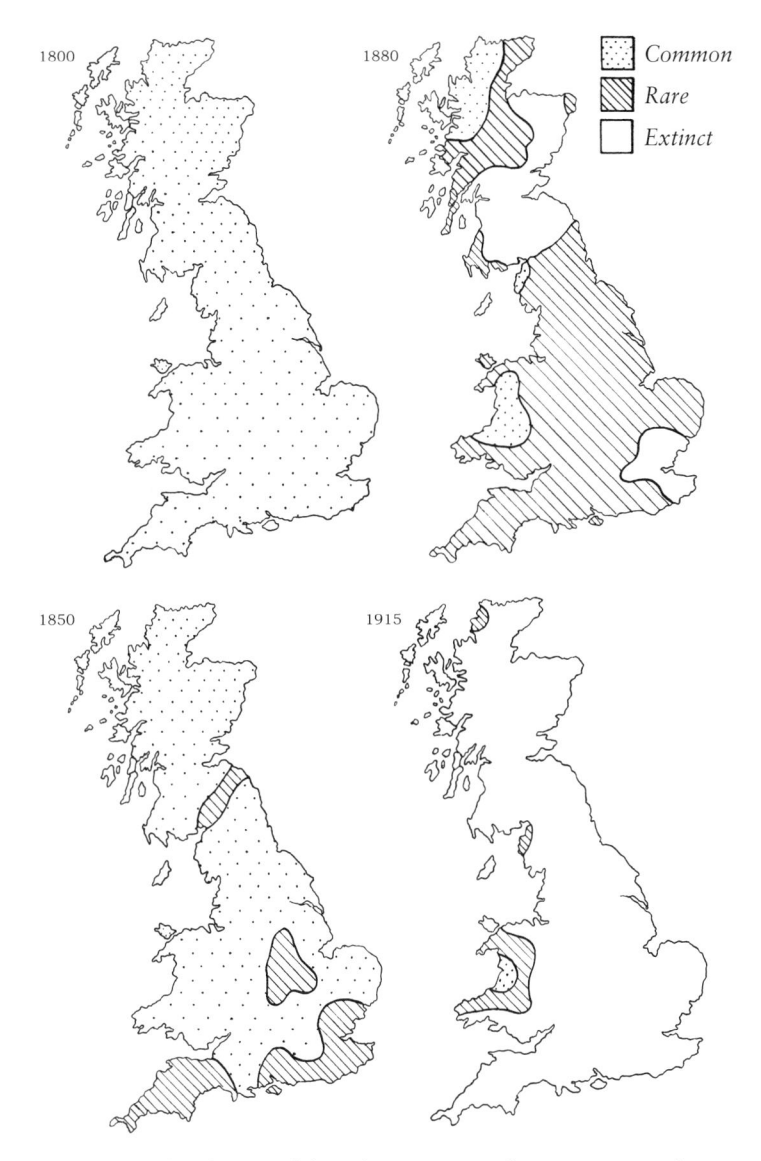

POLECATS | HOW WE NEARLY LOST THE POLECAT FROM BRITAIN

The changing distribution of the polecat in Britain between 1800 and 1915, showing the rapid contraction in range caused by culling associated with game shooting (redrawn from Langley and Yalden, 1977).

From today's perspective one is tempted to condemn such a damaging onslaught upon our fauna, but it is foolish to criticise those involved at the time because human attitudes were so very different then: in those days society placed no value upon predatory animals unless they were sporting quarry (such as the otter and fox) or had attractive fur (like the pine marten) – though neither of these 'values' necessarily guaranteed protection to populations. In those days neither ecological wisdom nor conservation ethics had crossed human synapses to enlighten our ancestors about the positive role of predators in ecosystems, nor about their intrinsic value as part of our native biodiversity and as thrilling creatures to admire and wonder at. For most people in late nineteenth-century Britain predators were simply a terrible nuisance and we were better off without them, so the gamekeepers were viewed at the time as doing a good job in removing them.

And what a devastating job they did! Increasingly organised culling of polecats by gamekeepers through the 1800s culminated in the four decades of 1870–1910, which stand out as the peak period for local extinctions with no fewer than 57 counties across Scotland, England and Wales losing their polecats as gamekeeper numbers climbed towards their 1911 peak. All this eradication effort was deployed primarily to ensure a sufficient abundance of two birds, one introduced and one native, that continue to dominate driven game shooting in Britain today: the pheasant (introduced originally from near the Black Sea in Georgia and Armenia, and later supplemented by the ring-necked pheasant from eastern China) was mainly reared and released to be shot on sporting estates in the lowlands; and the wild bred red grouse was shot over heather moorland in the uplands. These two mollycoddled birds have a lot to answer for in terms of the long-term impact of their defenders upon the distribution and abundance of predatory birds and mammals in Britain, for the polecat was but one of several predators pushed close to extinction between 1850 and 1914; a hundred years later all of them are still in recovery, with some doing better than others; the unfortunate Scottish wildcat is in intensive care and giving grave cause for concern.

Thankfully the ghastly onslaught on predators at the turn of the nineteenth and twentieth centuries was not sustained at its peak intensity for very long. The outbreak of the so-called 'Great War' of 1914–1918 marked a crucial turning point because many men involved in predator control left the land to fight in the trenches of northern Europe; subsequently the traditional sporting estates went into a steady decline, matched by numbers in the gamekeeping profession. Although it would be tasteless to celebrate the Great War for its surprising contribution to the conservation of British predators, it is fair to acknowledge its benign consequences: had Britain not joined the allied forces with such a heavy commitment of manpower in the early 1900s, then some predators such as the polecat would very likely have been driven to extinction and would probably still be absent from Britain today.

So the early decades of the twentieth century saw the polecat mainly confined to Wales, with possible remnant pockets hanging on elsewhere. Notably, polecats never quite disappeared from western parts of the English border counties of Shropshire and Herefordshire. Although the polecat survived in at least nine of the old counties of mainland Wales (Carmarthenshire, Pembrokeshire, Breconshire, Cardiganshire, Radnorshire, Montgomeryshire, Merionethshire, Denbighshire and Caernarvonshire), its presence was tenuous in many areas and its true stronghold in 1914 was described by Langley and Yalden as an area 'about 40 miles radius around Aberystwyth'; this was later corrected by subsequent authors, with Derek Yalden's blessing, to an historical stronghold of some 70 km (44 miles) radius around Aberdovey (which lies some 15 km north of Aberystwyth and is believed to reflect more closely the 'centre' of the stronghold). Why did polecats survive here better than anywhere else in Britain? Because government census data show that in 1911 it had a very low density of gamekeepers (0.2–0.8 gamekeepers per 1,000 hectares) compared with other parts of Britain; it also had a low human population density generally, so levels of persecution would have been relatively low during the most intensive period of predator culling. It is no coincidence that the red kite, another predator driven to the brink of extinction by persecution, survived in approximately the same area of mid Wales and nowhere else at the nadir of its fortunes in the early twentieth century.

One of the incidental pressures facing the polecat in parts of its precarious Welsh stronghold, even after the decline in gamekeeping pressure, was the rabbit-trapping industry. Largely because of the scarcity of most predators due to their culling by gamekeepers, in the first half of the twentieth century Britain was plagued by vast populations of wild rabbits; these in turn supported an industry based upon snaring rabbits for the sale of their meat and fur; thousands of wire snares were set out in the fields, and gangs of men gathered in the snared rabbits the next day and sent the carcasses on lorries and trains to the markets, even as far afield as London. This source of wild meat, whether bought at market or poached at night, sustained hungry Britons through lean times during the 1930s depression and the 1939–1945 World War. Once again this put polecats into direct competition with humans, this time for rabbits, with consequences that certainly hindered their recovery in the more rabbit-infested parts of Wales.

The presence of any predators such as foxes, stoats and polecats in the areas to be harvested for rabbits would undermine the snaring effort, because their night-time visits to the 'snaring fields' led to removal of or damage to the trapped rabbits (often held alive by the snares, so very tempting and easy prey) and thereby reduced the income from sales; so it became routine practice for the rabbit trappers to attempt to remove any predators in advance by any means they could. Inevitably, when *Myxomatosis* arrived and spread (with much human assistance) and killed more than 99 per cent of wild rabbits in the early 1950s, the rabbit-trapping industry collapsed immediately. Even when rabbit populations recovered in some areas we humans found we had lost our earlier taste for wild rabbit meat because of its association with such a visibly unpleasant disease.

Considering the likely indirect impact of *Myxomatosis* on polecats, the late Welsh naturalist Bill Condry observed that, far from suffering from the sudden loss of an abundant source of prey as one might expect, the polecat actually benefited more from the associated reduction in trapping pressure when intensive rabbit-trapping ceased. Clearly, like foxes, polecats were able to switch to alternative prey such as mice and voles during the rabbit-lean years of the 1950s, 60s and early 70s.

The beginnings of recovery in Wales
From the perspective of the conservation of predators like the polecat, human attitudes and activities in Britain improved in small, fitful steps

through the twentieth century. Following the 1914–1918 war, trapping pressure declined in line with the fall in numbers of gamekeepers and, later, where sporting estates persisted, trapping practice changed to a less intensive approach (being cheaper for the estate), so that fewer traps were deployed over shorter periods; and on many estates a greater reliance was placed upon rearing and releasing pheasants (rather than relying on wild-bred birds), with trapping concentrated around release pens rather than across the whole estate. Importantly, in 1958, the cruel and indiscriminate 'gin trap' became illegal and trappers had to use new 'spring traps' designed to kill small predators humanely, rather than just holding them by the legs in steel jaws as did the gin trap; there were new rules about setting spring traps inside tunnels to avoid harm to non-target species (hence the alternative name 'tunnel trap'); so there were laudable intentions to reduce both levels of suffering and the indiscriminate impact of traps, although achievements on these fronts have been rather limited in reality.

Signs of a modest recovery in polecat numbers in Wales were noticed by naturalists in the 1920s, confirming that persecution had been the main cause of the decline; yet the species remained so scarce in many areas as to be worth remarking upon whenever it was encountered (usually killed in a trap). Persecution continued, albeit at a reduced level, and not everyone was optimistic that polecats would survive: writing in 1921 Frances Pitt worried that 'The species still exists in some numbers in Cardiganshire, but how long it will be able to hold its own in the face of steady persecution is another matter'.

The Second World War (1939–1945) gave the polecat another valuable breathing space, with our attention focused on battling Hitler's forces across Europe rather than controlling predators at home. Soon afterwards William Taylor of the Forestry Commission (FC) undertook the first organised assessment of the polecat's occurrence on FC land across Wales in the period 1947–1950. His summary, published in 1952, was rather upbeat and optimistic: 'The species has undoubtedly profited by the reduced intensity of game preservation since 1914 and may be said to have taken a new lease of life, and the opportunity to increase its range, in most parts of the Principality with the exception of the county of Anglesey'.

Ken Walton was the first scientist to study polecats in Britain. Starting with a distribution survey in the period 1959–1962, he appealed widely for records of trap victims and road casualties so as to plot the species' range at the time. From 93 hectads (10 × 10 km squares) 312 records confirmed that polecats were found mainly in Wales, but also occurred in the border counties of Shropshire, Herefordshire and Gloucestershire (polecats were apparently lost from Gloucestershire about 1900, but probably reappeared in the county in the 1950s). Despite his widespread appeal, Ken Walton found no convincing evidence that polecats had survived elsewhere in England or in Scotland; this suggests that the small, remnant pockets occurring in 1915 in Sutherland and north Cumbria had probably fizzled out some time before the 1950s. This meant that, barring human intervention, the polecat's future in Britain would be solely dependent upon expansion from its Welsh stronghold, where recovery was already well under way by the early 1960s: writing in 1964 Walton described the species as 'common in the counties of Cardiganshire, Merionethshire, Montgomeryshire, Radnorshire, Caernarvonshire and south Denbighshire'.

'THANK HEAVEN FOR WALES!'

By the early 1960s polecats were also present, but less common and typically with restricted distributions, in other Welsh counties such as Carmarthenshire, Pembrokeshire, Breconshire, Monmouthshire and Flintshire; only Anglesey remained polecat-free, because of its island status, until the mid 1990s when Ken Walton (who had retired to live there) found road casualties close to the two bridges connecting Anglesey to the mainland. Glamorgan in the far south of Wales has been very slow to be recolonised: Ken Walton recorded one specimen there in his early 1960s survey, but not until the mid 1970s did polecats gain a true foothold in the rural north of the county; even in the late 1990s the VWT survey at the time suggested that polecats were still absent from most of the South Wales valleys; these represent the most industrialised and most densely populated area of Wales, with a high density of busy roads following the valley floors; it seems that polecats struggle to thrive in such a landscape.

Recolonisation of England
With the mountains and valleys of Wales and the English border counties providing the essential driving force, the polecat spread slowly but surely back into the English Midlands during the second half of the twentieth century. Advancing eastward like a secret black and tan tide, polecats reappeared in Worcestershire in the 1960s; in Cheshire, Staffordshire and possibly Warwickshire in the 1970s; in Northamptonshire in the 1980s; and in Derbyshire, Oxfordshire and Leicestershire in the 1990s. By the end of the 1990s the polecat's natural spread had re-established it widely once again in the western Midlands of England. Apart from a big gap based upon the West Midlands conurbation (not very good polecat habitat), it enjoyed an unbroken English distribution from the southern fringes of Manchester in the north down to the Stroud/Cirencester area of Gloucestershire in the south; and from the Welsh borders in the west across to the western fringes of the Peak District and western parts of Leicestershire, Northamptonshire and Oxfordshire in the east. Thereafter the pattern of spread in England is confused by the occurrence of translocated polecats and their offspring established in the wild beyond the limits of their naturally expanding range (see the section on reintroductions on page 42). By the late 1990s these new populations were established in Hertfordshire, Bedfordshire, south Buckinghamshire,

south-east Oxfordshire, north Berkshire, Hampshire, Wiltshire and Cumbria.

Much of the polecat's natural recolonisation of England up to the 1990s was not tracked closely at the time because those involved in recording mammals, mindful of the written guidance on distribution that typically described the species as being 'confined to Wales and one or two border counties', tended to err on the side of caution and classified any true polecats found well outside of Wales as 'probable polecat-ferrets'. A big contributory factor in this process was the widespread lack of familiarity with the features of a true polecat among biological recorders in England, and among naturalists generally, so that confidence in correct identification was as rare as the polecat itself had been some fifty years earlier. Thus, due to this understandably conservative approach to recording, many exciting specimens were misclassified and lurked like second-class citizens deep in museum freezers until I came calling on behalf of the VWT polecat project in the early 1990s. One of my more pleasant tasks was to help the English naturalist community, county by county, to realise that a native carnivore, missing for a hundred years or more, had recently re-joined the local mammal list. Such 'good news' stories were rightly celebrated in local media across the English Midlands, and in Northamptonshire naturalists were so keen to celebrate that in January 1995 they held a very jolly 'Welcome Back the Polecat' party.

In order to understand and plot accurately the pattern of polecat recovery in Britain I needed to tease apart the relative contributions to the polecat's late 1990s distribution of three processes operating before and after the previous distribution map in 1991: firstly the unrecorded pre-1991 natural range expansion (due to 'conservative recording'); secondly the natural range expansion since 1991 recorded by the VWT; and finally the reintroduction of polecats leading to the establishment of new populations, some of which were present but not recorded before 1991. My head-scratching and careful number-crunching suggested that each process contributed approximately one third to the extent of apparent range expansion between 1991 and 1997 (when the VWT survey finished).

Having corrected for the influence of 'conservative recording' on apparent natural range expansion, I was able to draw crude wiggly lines on maps to reconstruct the shifting fronts of the polecat's expanding range at intervals from the 1960s through to the mid 1990s. These revealed some interesting patterns: notably that eastward expansion of the polecat's range was very slow up to the mid 1970s (perhaps because rabbits were still scarce following the effects of *Myxomatosis*?); thereafter in England the front moved eastward at an average rate of 3.5 kilometres per year up to the mid 1980s; then increased to 4.3 kilometres per year up to the mid 1990s. This increasing rate of range expansion may have many causes, not least the fuelling effect of the post-*Myxomatosis* recovery of rabbit numbers since the 1970s, as well as the generally richer base of prey available to polecats in the English lowlands compared with the mountains of Wales. Finally, it seemed that the polecat's eastward advance south of Birmingham occurred about ten years ahead of that to the north of Birmingham; this may simply be because, at the polecat's nadir in the early 1900s, more animals survived in the sparsely populated hills of west Herefordshire and south-west Shropshire than did further north, so giving a slight head start to expansion in the southern part of the species' range as soon as the trapping pressure eased up.

Polecats in Scotland?

The polecat probably became extinct in Scotland sometime between 1915 and 1950, but there have been several attempted reintroductions since then (see the section on reintroductions on the next page) with either moderate, temporary or uncertain success. The VWT's 1990s polecat survey recorded the species in only eight Scottish hectads, all in Argyll (thanks to the recording efforts of local naturalist Clive Craik), which must have arisen from an earlier introduction. However, there was no evidence of this population surviving during the VWT's 2000s survey, when nine polecats were recorded from just six Scottish hectads in Perthshire (2), Caithness (2), Sutherland (1) and Lanark (1). The Perthshire and Lanarkshire records relate to known recent releases (and the Perthshire animals appear to have had fun with feral ferrets, as some specimens here were classed as polecat-ferrets); but the 2000s Sutherland and Caithness records (five polecat specimens in total) are of unknown origin because no reintroduction has been reported from this far northern part of Scotland.

While statistical analysis suggests that an unreported release is the most likely explanation for the presence of polecats in the far north of Scotland, for the irrepressible optimist there is a tantalising alternative origin for these animals: their current proximity to the small pocket of polecat presence surviving in Sutherland in 1915 (modern records lie less than 100 kilometres to the east) and the very sparse human population in that part of Scotland (meaning that an equally sparse polecat population might perhaps be overlooked for decades) makes it just feasible that polecats persisted unnoticed through the twentieth century; in which case the specimens examined in the early 2000s could represent valuable modern relics of the polecat's former Scottish population. Exciting work for any mammal recorders and geneticists who can get their hands on more recent specimens!

Another issue in Scotland is the long-standing occurrence of feral polecat-ferrets on some offshore islands, where the local inhabitants sometimes refer to them as 'polecats'. Following the escape, abandonment or deliberate release of captive animals in the past, several parts of the Inner and Outer Hebrides and Shetland still support self-sustaining feral polecat-ferret populations that have been present for many decades. On Islay and parts of Shetland ferrets were released in the 1970s and 1980s in the mistaken belief that they would control wild rabbit populations. Some long-established island populations, such as those on Mull, appear quite dark and polecat-like despite their known ferrety origins.

The role of reintroductions

Polecats, like ferrets, breed very readily in captivity, which means that anyone keeping animals of both genders together is likely to end up with a surplus each autumn, intentionally or otherwise. Wild-caught or captive-bred polecats of uncertain origin have been translocated and released into various parts of Britain since the 1960s, usually by people motivated to restore populations to areas from which polecats were missing because of historical persecution. These releases have generally been done privately and covertly, and regrettably some have been neither well planned nor followed up by effective monitoring to find out whether they succeeded or failed and why. Because of their secretive nature it has not been easy to gather even basic information about such releases; the following is a list of the known release areas with dates (there are bound to be others):

Location	Period of releases	Number of animals	Outcome
Cumbria	1960s–1980s	150+	Established population (but high proportion of polecat-ferrets)
Argyll	1970s	Unknown	Failed?
Loch Ness	1982	Unknown	Failed?
Hertfordshire	1980s–1990s	40–50	Merged with expanding native range
South Bucks/Oxon/Berks	1980s	Unknown	Merged with expanding native range
Hampshire/Wiltshire	Early 1990s?	Unknown	Merged with expanding native range
Perthshire	1990s	Unknown	Established population (but high proportion of polecat-ferrets)
Scottish Borders	2000s	Unknown	Unknown

Collectively these reintroduction efforts can claim only limited success at best: most of the polecat's range expansion in Britain since the 1920s has arisen through natural spread, which has now overtaken all the reintroduced populations in the southern half of England; only the Cumbrian reintroduction, which involved the release of a large number of polecats over several years, has led to the establishment of a new population that expanded slowly into adjacent counties; the outcome of the various Scottish ones is less certain, although a population appears to be established in Perthshire. One characteristic of these outlying reintroduced populations in northern England and Scotland is a relatively high proportion of animals with 'ferrety' features, indicating that the released animals interbred with escaped or feral ferrets.

In the absence of a public record of both the release methods used and monitoring of animals post-release, we are left to wonder why some polecat reintroductions in Britain have succeeded and some have failed. Many things can go wrong with a release programme, especially if it is not meticulously planned: if the release site already supports wild polecats the released animals will face tough competition and may fail to establish territories; if sources of prey are inadequate or mortality risks are high (e.g. trapping pressure on shooting estates or a high density of busy roads) then released animals may lose condition, suffer injuries or die; if feral ferrets are present cross-breeding may reduce the fitness of the population; finally, many studies of other mammals have shown that captive-bred animals tend not to survive and establish populations in the wild post-release as successfully as wild-caught ones.

On the monitoring of releases question, the single glowing exception is the RSPCA's study of the release of wild polecats cared for at its Stapeley Grange Wildlife Centre in Cheshire. Growing numbers of injured adults or orphaned wild polecats are taken there each year (137 in total between 1997 and 2008, for example); all those fit enough are 'soft-released' into the wild, when the time is right (usually the autumn), at carefully chosen locations where their chances of survival are greatest. To improve understanding of how the animals fared, between 2005 and 2008 the RSPCA radio-tracked 32 released polecats and published their findings. After fourteen days 81 per cent of polecats were still alive, and a minimum of 50 per cent were alive after one month; 22 per cent shed their radio collars (not unusual in studies of wild polecats); 12 per cent were killed by vehicles during the radio-tracking and a further 16 per cent were run over and killed months later (again this is not unusual). So these wild-born polecats that had spent some time in captivity probably fared little worse than naturally dispersing wild polecats, in which mortality is quite high before the animals settle in territories of their own.

At the time of writing in 2015 there are reports of further private releases of captive-bred polecats into central, south-east or eastern England where the species is either already well established or poised to establish imminently through natural spread. This makes little sense to me and I worry about the welfare of the animals post-release: it seems wrong to put 'soft' captive-bred polecats, which we know are disadvantaged compared with wild-bred ones, into areas where they are very likely to fail in competition with the much more vigorous wild animals in established populations.

Current distribution and future spread

The VWT continues to monitor the polecat's changing distribution, and there is abundant evidence that the late twentieth-century range expansion in southern Britain has continued into the new millennium. Apart from the big urban areas in which polecats fail to establish populations, the species now has an unbroken distribution from the coasts of West Wales across to rural Essex and Surrey either side of London; and from the fringes of the south Pennine conurbations down to the south coast of England. Beyond this main block lie the outlier populations in Scotland and north-west England, with new reports of polecats from parts of Devon, Cornwall and East Kent.

With the erstwhile 'Polecat Mother Ship' Wales now fully repopulated, the only options for further expansion lie in Scotland and England, with the latter most likely to contribute initially simply because there is a much greater existing population in England providing a 'head of steam' to fuel expansion here compared with Scotland. Range expansion is now advancing down the south-west peninsula, with polecats heading westward through Somerset and Dorset into Devon; to the south of London polecats are moving eastward through Surrey and Sussex towards Kent; and further north the polecat is expanding eastward into the flat lands and fens of East Anglia. Of course, we should temper any assumptions about untrammelled expansion with caveats about adequate prey populations and sustainable mortality; and we must always be aware that elusive species like the polecat, whilst remaining widespread, may suffer local declines in response to changes in habitat and mortality factors – hence the importance of monitoring both distribution *and* abundance. Nevertheless, this is thrilling news for the many naturalists in southern Britain who doubted they would ever see the return of such a long-lost mammal as the polecat.

One constraint to northward expansion in England appears to be the block of polecat-unfriendly habitat comprising large conurbations, upland areas and transport links across northern England between Liverpool and the Humber estuary. For example, despite being present in Cheshire and Staffordshire since the 1970s, and in Derbyshire since the 1990s, midland polecats have struggled to spread northwards through this block into south Lancashire and West and South Yorkshire beyond. So any polecat recovery in northern England would depend either upon expansion of the reintroduced population in Cumbria or upon polecats spreading through or around the Liverpool to Humber 'blockage'; one likely route lies to the east of Doncaster, where polecats from Derbyshire and Nottinghamshire could spread north through low-lying rural landscapes into Lincolnshire and South Yorkshire.

The polecat's distribution in Britain in 2014, showing how much of its former range it has recolonised over the preceding 100 years.

THE POLECAT'S STATUS IN EUROPE

In contrast with the optimistic picture of our polecat's recovery and range expansion in Britain, things seem much less rosy across the water on the European Continent: through my mustelid contacts I have heard reports of actual or possible population declines since the mid twentieth century from Italy, Spain, Denmark, Belgium, France, Lithuania, the Netherlands, Belarus, Poland, Germany and Luxembourg. Where likely causes are identified, these have usually involved reductions in prey populations (e.g. rabbits disappearing due to viral haemorrhagic disease), loss of habitat (e.g. drainage of wetlands) and competition with invasive populations of feral American mink. On the IUCN's Red List the European polecat is currently in the category of 'Least Concern'. However, the suggestions of a widespread decline on the Continent is prompting a rethink on this; although any change in the IUCN's listing has to be based on sound evidence, which may not be available for many countries because the polecat is not a well-studied species.

SIZE, SHAPE AND COLOUR

Most people, including most naturalists, have never had a good close-up view of a live, wild polecat; the great majority of our encounters are with the gory carcasses of road casualties in various states of battery and putrefaction; some are lucky enough to have glimpsed a live polecat in car headlights crossing a road at night, but these encounters are brief and unpredictable, with no opportunity to dwell on the features that make the polecat distinctive. Furthermore, good photographic images of polecats are few and far between, and many of them are of captive animals with 'ferrety' features, so they are unreliable guides to what true polecats look like.

During my time studying wild polecats with the VWT I was in the privileged position of live-trapping and releasing many of them (under licences from the relevant government agencies), so I have probably seen more live, wild polecats close-up than almost anyone else in Britain today. Before offering a description of a typical polecat, it is important to understand the nature and origins of variations in appearance: like many mammals polecats look different in their summer and winter pelage states, with animals in winter looking paler and woollier than in their sleek dark summer coats; kits and juveniles look different from adults; male polecats are much larger than females, with some noticeable differences in body shape, such as broader heads and thicker necks in males; there are slight geographical variations in pelage colour linked to the influence of interbreeding with ferrets, with animals furthest from Wales more likely to have pale hints of ferret in their pelage; and finally there are genetically recessive fur colours – erythrism and albinism – that are encountered only rarely in wild populations.

Size and shape

Like so many of their weasely relatives, polecats have elongated bodies with a small, flattish head, short legs and modest tails. They are larger and chunkier than stoats and weasels, but their bodies still resemble a sinuous cylinder that is perfectly adapted to exploring burrows and other tight spaces where prey might be found. Despite the name, there is nothing very cat-like about the polecat: its ears are small and rounded, the body size is smaller and the legs and tail much shorter than a cat's. The polecat is very similar in size and shape to the American mink, though the latter is slightly less heavily built.

One striking polecat feature is the 'sexual dimorphism' of body size, with males being much larger than females: at its most extreme a big adult male (the heaviest wild polecats I ever saw were males weighing just over

Cat, polecat and mink, showing relative sizes.

2,000 grams, but the average was about 1,440 grams) may be more than three times the weight of a small adult female (which may be as little as 500 grams, but occasionally up to 1,000 grams); on average the male: female bodyweight ratio is 1.6–1.8, which is more extreme than in other small mustelids. The reason for this great difference lies in the brutality of polecat love-making and the need for single mothers to keep their energetic costs down: males need to be bigger and stronger than females in order to catch and restrain them during mating; and males compete for receptive females by fighting, which provides an extra incentive to be big and strong; conversely the females, which rear their young without any paternal help, face pressures to stay small, minimising their own energy needs so as to provide as much food as possible for their kits.

These different reproductive roles also explain some marked seasonal bodyweight and shape changes in polecats: fuelled by hormones in preparation for the rigours of the mating season, males put on weight over winter to reach peak fighting condition in March, when their necks are thick and very muscular; after their mating and fighting exertions, from April to June, they are in poorest condition with visibly slimmer necks in mid summer; females also put on weight over winter but lose condition later than the males, being lightest from July to September, due to the demands of rearing, feeding and protecting their young through the summer. During the VWT study I was able to catch the same polecats at intervals over a year or more so I observed these changes in individual animals: one male called George (after gamekeeper George Barford – most of my polecats were named after characters in *The Archers* in the 1990s) was a heavy-necked bruiser of 1,540 grams in late February, with large, taut testes and a thick winter coat; three months later, after the mating season, he had shrunk to a freshly scarred 1,200 gram shadow of his former self, with small, flaccid testes and a short summer coat that revealed his newly slimline neck.

As well as the gender and seasonal differences in body size there seem to be some geographical ones too. For example, adult polecats measured in the VWT's study in lowland England in the 1990s tended to be longer and heavier on average than those in Philip Blandford's study in the hills of mid Wales in the 1980s. This was true for both genders, with lowland females on average 4 millimetres longer and 98 grams heavier than their upland sisters; and lowland males on average 44 millimetres longer and 328 grams heavier than their upland brothers. These differences are probably environmental rather than genetic in origin: they are very likely a consequence of the greater range and biomass of prey available to polecats in the English lowlands compared with upland Wales, enabling lowland juveniles to achieve a greater body size than upland ones. For the polecat, it seems that life really is richer in the 'soft underbelly' of the lowlands and this is reflected in the greater body size they can achieve.

	mean total length	mean weight
Adult males in mid Wales	547 mm	1,111 g
Adult males in lowland England	591 mm	1,439 g
Adult females in mid Wales	500 mm	689 g
Adult females in lowland England	504 mm	787 g

Skeletal stuff
Starting at the front end, the polecat has a fairly flat and robust skull with a short braincase and typical carnivorous dentition: the dental formula for permanent teeth in adults is 2(I3/3 C1/1 P3/3 M1/2) = 34, which translates as each side of the jaws having three upper and three lower incisors, one upper and one lower canine, three upper and three lower premolars, and one upper and two lower molars, amounting to 34 teeth; the formula for deciduous teeth in juveniles, which don't have the six molars found in adults, is 2(I3/3 C1/1 P3/3) = 28. Some adult wild polecats have supernumerary (extra) incisors, especially in the upper row, which might possibly be a reflection of ferret genes.

As explained in the section on *Ferret Origins and Domestication*, one of the polecat's skull characteristics – the post-orbital constriction – was the focus of early debate about the identity of the ferret's wild ancestor. The same 'waist' feature was measured by naturalists in the mistaken belief that one could reliably separate the skulls of polecats and ferrets on the basis of the differing widths of their post-orbital constrictions, with the ferret having the narrower one; then Andrew Kitchener revealed that the shape is strongly influenced by environmental factors during skull development, making it effectively useless as a distinguishing feature.

After the skull, the next most exciting feature in the polecat's otherwise unremarkable skeleton is the baculum or penis bone. Unlike we human males, who rely on the dodgy merits of hydrostatic pressure to help us perform, most mammals have opted for a simple bone and muscle system to achieve penetration. In polecats the baculum is a slim and delicately curved bone with an expanded knobbly base (where the muscles attach), a tapering shaft and a hooked tip. Curiously the polecat baculum is asymmetrical, curving slightly to the right near the tip when viewed from above. Aware of changes in baculum length and weight through a polecat's life, Ken Walton explored the possibility of using these measures as an indicator of age (albeit only dead polecats, and males only!); he coyly observed 'in older animals the bone continues to increase in weight, but not in length, owing mainly to the addition of basal knobs'; he also found that, for any given weight, the polecat baculum is 10 – 11 mm longer than a ferret baculum so, in its troubled relations with the polecat, the unfortunate male ferret has to endure 'baculum envy' on top of all its other woes.

Colouration

Starting at the very front of its strikingly marked face, the polecat has a rhinarium that is dark brown or reddish brown (a pale brown or pink rhinarium is a ferrety feature); almost encircling its nose and mouth is a band of bright white fur on the chin and muzzle, broken only by a strip of dark brown-black fur on the top of the muzzle that connects the rhinarium with the dark facial mask above (where the white fur fully encircles the muzzle so there is no dark fur connection with the rhinarium, this is viewed as a ferrety feature, although in south-east Poland – where there is no history of ferreting because there are no rabbits – I have seen museum polecat specimens with no 'dark connection' above the rhinarium); on the chin the white fur does not extend onto the throat, which is near-black (if it does, with a yellowish throat extension or patches of yellowish fur on the throat, this is a ferrety feature).

The remainder of the polecat's face is covered by a bold pattern of dark and light fur: blackish-brown fur across the eyes forms a 'bandit mask' (sometimes with a tiny tuft of pale fur beside the inner edge of each eye), which is surrounded by a seasonally variable pattern of greyish-white fur that is most extensive in the winter coat, when a broad pale 'frontal band' extends across the forehead and may link via the cheeks with the white fur of the chin and muzzle to form a complete ring; in summer this pale ring is greatly reduced and fragmented into limited patches between the eyes and ears by dark fur on the forehead and below the eyes; the margins of the short ears are covered in whitish fur in both summer and winter pelage. The overall effect is an attention-grabbing 'look at me!' face that serves as a memorable warning to potential aggressors foolish enough to test the polecat's pungent defences.

Behind its startlingly marked face the polecat's colouration is dusky and calm, although there is some patterning and seasonal variation arising from the interplay between the two types of hair that make up its coat – the soft, pale woolly underfur and the longer, stiffer near-black guard hairs: in the winter coat the underfur is longer (25 mm as compared with 15 mm), denser and whiter than in summer, but it remains greyish on the limbs, shoulders, rump and tail so these areas look darker; the guard hairs vary from dark brown to an iridescent purplish-black and tend to be darkest on the throat, chest, limbs and tail; in winter the guard hairs on the body are longer and pale towards their base, giving a lighter colour to the body, especially when the dense, creamy white underfur prevents the dark guard hairs from lying flat as they tend to do in the summer pelage. So, rather like Siamese cats, polecats in winter have dark extremities but may look very pale on the body (especially noticeable when the creamy-white underfur is illuminated in car headlights) and this may provide camouflage in snowy landscapes – perhaps offering protection against potential nocturnal predators such as large owls.

One complication arising from the polecat's paler winter coat and its more extensive pale facial markings is that, because polecat-ferrets tend to be paler than true polecats, these features lead some people to wonder whether the animal they have found is really a polecat; so it is important to understand the seasonal differences between the pelage states. Polecats in their dark summer coats are more likely to be mistaken for American mink, which are very similar in size and shape but with no pale fur above the lips. Occasionally naturalists have brought me a dead mink or shown me a photograph of one, so I've had to explain why their mink was actually a polecat in summer coat (the polecat's whitish muzzle and ear tips are the best giveaway).

Quantifying colour variations in polecats

One of many important contributions made by Andrew Kitchener to our understanding of polecat biology is his development of a simple system for scoring polecat pelts based on variations in the colouration of fur between 'true polecat' specimens and those with ferrety features. Andrew identified ten 'pelage characters' that were scored on a scale from 1 (= pale and ferrety) to 3 (= dark and polecatty); and the resultant 'pelage character total' (PCT) was a score on a scale from 30 (purest polecat) to 10 (most ferrety). In reality, and because individual and seasonal variations in pelage even among true polecats affect some pelage character scores, polecat populations tended to have average scores in the mid to high 20s, while populations of feral ferrets on Scottish Islands, for example, had average scores of about 18 or 19.

The PCT system has been useful in examining geographical variations in the occurrence of ferrety features within the polecat's expanding British range. Based upon specimens collected by naturalists since the 1950s, and including those from the VWT's 1990s distribution survey, there was a decline in average PCT scores from west to east: polecat populations in Wales had an average PCT score of 26.5 (with individual polecat scores ranging from 23 to 30); those in Herefordshire and Shropshire had an average PCT of 26.6 (thereby confirming the status of these two English border counties as an integral part of the Welsh hotspot of polecat 'purity'); those further away from mid Wales in Gloucestershire, Worcestershire, Staffordshire and Cheshire scored lower with an average PCT of 25.51; while those further east again in Berkshire, Oxfordshire, Northamptonshire, Warwickshire and Derbyshire were lower still with an average PCT of 25.24.

Alongside the west-east decline in average PCT, there is a predictable tendency for the proportion of obviously ferrety specimens with low PCT scores to increase from west to east: for example, in the 1990s samples gathered by the VWT, the proportion of ferret-like specimens rises from just 2.2 per cent in Wales, to 24.0 per cent in the East Midlands.

These geographical trends in colouration suggest an increasing tendency for polecats to mate with feral ferrets as the population has expanded eastward across central England; this is not surprising because young male polecats probably disperse further than females and, consequently, around the fringes of the species' expanding range pioneering males risk finding themselves in a desperate 'polecat love void' where their only mating opportunities lie with the local ferrets. In simple terms the blackest polecats will probably survive best in the wild, so this eastward 'blonding' trend might be expected to fade away as more true polecats spread eastward. I suspect the late and hugely talented Amy Winehouse was a polecat fan who appreciated the potential threat arising from breeding with ferrets: her fine 2006 album *Back to Black* is clearly a rallying cry to all polecats to safeguard their pure dusky phenotype by resisting the blonde temptations offered by ferrets.

There is already evidence that English polecats have got Amy's tuneful message: in Lauren Harrington's Oxfordshire study in the mid 2000s she undertook PCT scoring of the wild polecats she trapped; all had PCT scores of between 22 and 27, indicating a good level of polecat 'purity'; also she found fewer low-scoring (i.e. ferrety) individuals than had been recorded in the same area in the 1990s; on this basis Lauren suggested that genetic introgression (the posh phrase for hybridisation) with feral ferrets was decreasing in her study area. This evidence is backed up by the VWT's second distribution survey covering 2004–2006, which revealed that the percentage of obviously ferrety specimens in Oxfordshire was less than 3 per cent. This evidence enables us to be quietly optimistic about the future integrity of wild polecats in Britain, with the common occurrence of 'ferrety' specimens perhaps only a temporary feature of the early stages of recolonisation.

Some of the fur colour differences between true polecats and ferrety ones are rather subjective and prone to seasonal variation, with polecats generally much the darker of the two, for example. However, there are a few tell-tale features to look out for (illustrated neatly in the VWT's free leaflet *Polecats and Ferrets: How to tell them apart*); these are described in the table on the next page. Note that not all of the ferrety features will appear in every ferrety specimen.

True polecat features	'Ferrety' features
Rhinarium dark or reddish brown	Rhinarium pale brown or pinkish
Dark fur extending down top of muzzle connects strongly with rhinarium	Weak or no connection between rhinarium and dark fur on top of muzzle, or white fur fully encircles muzzle
Short white chin patch (< 60 mm long)	White chin patch has yellowish extension onto throat (> 60 mm long) and/or yellow spots or patches on throat
Fur colour on top of feet and toes is blackish	Some fur on the top of feet and toes is yellowish-white
Guard hairs on hindquarters and tail are all blackish	Guard hairs on hindquarters and tail include a thin scatter of whitish individual hairs
Pale cheek patches and frontal band contrast with dark facial mask	Pale cheek patches and frontal ban extensive and contrast poorly with darker facial mask

Non-subjective pelage characters that separate true polecats from those with ferrety features.

Rare colour morphs

Like most mammals, polecat populations occasionally produce individuals with a genetically recessive fur colour. Erythristic or 'red' polecats, in which the blackish pigment in the guard hairs is replaced by a ginger one, turn up very infrequently in Britain, though I suspect they are under-recorded because their ginger-brown colouring may lead people to mistake them for oddly coloured ferrets. This form was first reported from Wales in 1903, and most records up until the 1950s were from a mainly coastal area of West Wales; since then Ken Walton saw only one in the 1960s (in Montgomeryshire); through my work with the VWT I encountered three in the 1990s (one in Carmarthenshire and two in Oxfordshire) and three in the period 2004–2006 (in Brecknock, Radnorshire and Cheshire).

Albino polecats must occur in wild populations from time to time, as they do in many other species, but would we recognise them as such when we are predisposed to assume that any blond, polecat-shaped specimen with pink eyes is an escaped or feral ferret, especially if it is a road casualty carcass not exhibiting much polecat-like behaviour!? Even though wild albino polecats occurred often enough to be the probable source of the domestic ferret two thousand years ago, I suspect today we misidentify almost all of them for the reason given above. I have heard of only two probable wild albino polecats in the period 1993–2006 (with a third from the VWT's survey in 2014–2015): one was recovered from the wild as a fierce orphan kit in Hampshire; and the other was photographed as a kit in a Cheshire garden with a normal coloured mother and siblings.

Some mammal populations produce a melanistic form, in which the normal guard hairs are replaced with black ones, but in polecats this colour variation is hard to envisage because the normal colour of most guard hairs is already near-black. Nevertheless, in France Thierry Lodé has reported a dark, mink-like form of polecat that he suggests may be an example of melanism; I have never seen one of these in Britain.

Fighting and mating scars – the white tufts of passion!
When scars heal on a polecat's skin some of the guard hairs grow back as white instead of the usual dark brown or purplish-black, so as an animal ages it accumulates lasting signs of previous injuries, which are mostly inflicted by other polecats during fighting or mating. Old male polecats, for example, may have many small tufts and flecks of white hairs on both sides of their necks arising from the sites of bites inflicted during fights with other males, giving the fur here a grizzled look. Old females show a similar effect on the back of their necks where the males grip the skin with the teeth during mating. In the absence of other ways of ageing animals, these 'badges of passion' are a useful way of separating older polecats from those that have not yet lived through the hectic violence of a mating season.

POLECAT SENSES

Like so many solitary, nocturnal mammals the polecat inhabits a rich sensory world that we relatively 'sense-numb' humans struggle to comprehend. Although it has moderate eyesight – reportedly functioning relatively better at night than in daylight – the polecat relies mainly upon its acute senses of hearing and smell to find prey, to identify mates, neighbours and enemies, and to avoid dangerous places and situations. Polecats are remarkably good at locating slight noises very accurately – a handy skill if one's life depends upon detecting small prey such as mice, voles or frogs in thick undergrowth – and their reactions to sound are lightning-fast to maximise the chances of a successful capture.

An acute sense of smell enables the polecat to follow the scent trails left by its prey; and scent may influence prey selection where individuals have developed a preference for certain species. Olfaction (smells and smelling) is also an important part of polecat social life, enabling animals to exchange scented messages without ever meeting face to face (see *Communication*, page 65).

I learnt a lot about the relative importance of polecat senses during a memorable encounter one calm, moonlit night in Herefordshire: I was radio-tracking a male polecat foraging busily along a thick, rabbit-infested hedgerow between two pasture fields below a small wood; so as not to disturb him I stood in a field with my aerial and receiver some thirty metres from the hedge, listening to the high-pitched bleeps from his radio collar on the receiver, with a gentle breeze carrying my scent away to the wood behind me. Expecting the polecat to continue hunting along the hedge, I was surprised when the ever-louder bleeping indicated that he had left the hedge and was getting closer to me. I soon saw him bounding over the tight-grazed, moonlit turf in a direct line towards me. With aerial aloft I froze as he stopped some five metres away, with the space between us filled by the screaming bleeps from the receiver. As I imagined my polecat wondering how the oddly shaped tree had grown so suddenly in the open field and what strange animal was making the bleeping noises halfway up the trunk, it dawned on me that he must have heard 'his' radio bleeps on my receiver from thirty metres away and had decided to investigate in case it led him to some tasty new prey. His eyesight was not

PHOTOGRAPHS BY RICHARD BOWLER

This alert polecat reminds us how much the animals rely on their senses for survival: the ears, eyes and nose are perfectly aligned and all are used to different degrees to detect potential prey and sources of danger; and the long whiskers may play a part in exploring burrows in the dark.

Polecats in Continental Europe typically forage in wetland habitats because of their reliance upon amphibians as prey. In Britain there is no such association because wild rabbits are their most important prey, but they do sometimes visit ponds to feast on spawning frogs and toads in the spring.

The end of a successful hunt! This polecat is feasting on a piece of its favourite prey – wild rabbit – that may comprise over 80 per cent of the polecat's diet in Britain.

The polecat has long sharp claws that are used during foraging and help it to restrain large prey such as rabbits.

In summer coat a polecat may appear so dark in colour that, if you don't get a clear view of the pale markings on the face and ear tips, it can easily be mistaken for an American mink.

A foraging polecat is intensely inquisitive and finds any hole or burrow quite irresistible!

A long, slim and sinuous body enables a polecat to explore all sorts of burrows, tunnels and pipes in search of prey and safe resting sites.

The polecat's bold facial markings are the most striking feature of its otherwise nondescript appearance. They serve as a warning to potential predators that it has defensive weapons at both ends: sharp teeth at the front and a pungent stink at the rear!

This male polecat is in his summer coat, showing the much darker body colour, the characteristic 'bandit mask' and the more restricted pale facial markings compared with the winter coat.

In mid-winter polecats show reduced levels of activity and spend more time resting in their dens. But they emerge to forage most nights, even when there is snow on the ground.

A rabbit's-eye view of a hunting polecat at a burrow entrance. The predator uses its keen sense of smell to establish whether the burrow is occupied or not.

Foraging for fresh-killed carrion on roads at night can be fatal for the polecat. Road casualties like this one are most common in the autumn; they are good evidence that polecats are well established in an area so are often used as the basis for distribution surveys.

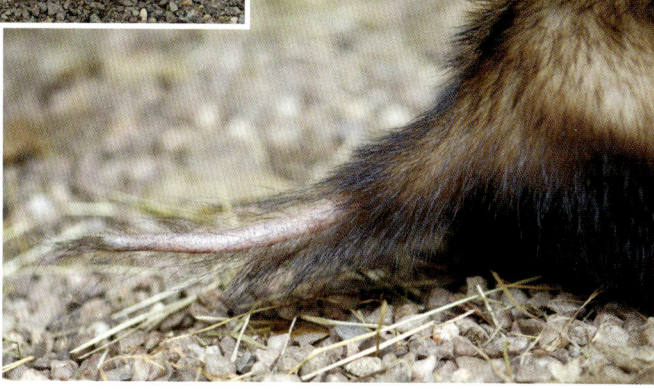

This polecat has a partly bald tail because of a harmless form of alopecia (hair loss) that affects some animals, usually males, during the summer months. Affected animals don't appear to suffer and the fur regrows normally when they moult into their winter coats.

At one of our wildlife feeding stations I built a shallow pool so that I could take reflection photos of visiting animals. My trail cam showed the local hedgehog population was coming to feed, but there was also the occasional visit from a polecat. As autumn turned to winter, the hedgehogs hibernated and the polecat's visits increased until he was visiting every night.

I set up a DSLR camera trap consisting of a PIR motion sensor that fires my camera and flashes when movement is sensed. I always run a trail cam alongside the DSLR camera trap to begin with to assess the animal's reaction to the flashes and the noise of the camera shutter. The polecat wasn't fazed in the slightest; most nights taking between 50 and 100 images of himself.

When using a camera trap, getting the animal in focus can be tricky. To achieve this, many of the images were taken with a 15 mm wide angle lens set at an aperture of F14 to give a big depth of field; shutter speed was set manually at 250th of a second with 3 flashes used to light the image. These were set at 1/16th power. It was the quick burst of light that froze the polecat in the image rather than the shutter speed.

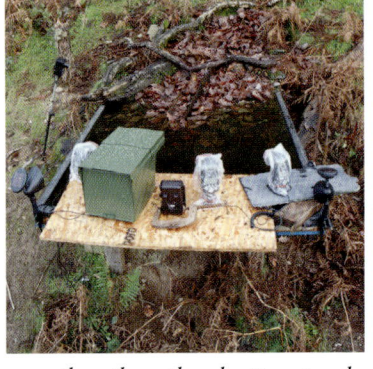

The polecat did not visit us during the summer, so I would like to thank the Chestnut Centre Otter, Owl and Wildlife Park in Chapel-en-le-Frith, Derbyshire, for inviting me to photograph their polecats in their summer coats.

Richard Bowler has had a passion for the natural world all his life. During his twenties he was fortunate enough to travel to remote and unspoilt parts of Africa, South and Central America. Usually with a fishing rod in tow, Richard started taking a camera along to capture the beauty of the natural world he was seeing in places like the Amazon or Zambezi valley. Today, the camera has taken over from the fishing rod.

Richard lives with his partner Helen and their menagerie of animals on a remote smallholding in the Berwyns, North Wales.

His photographs have appeared in many national newspapers, magazines and books, and he showcases his latest images on his Twitter and Facebook accounts. Richard's website is www.richardbowlerwildlifephotography.com.

good enough to identify me as a hazard; but as he circled round me to locate the source of the bleeps he got a whiff of my scent and bolted into the woodland.

So the polecat's nose and ears are the key to its survival, with eyesight a lower ranking but not wholly unimportant sense; and after my 'frozen tree' encounter I always wore headphones to stop the radio bleeps from interfering with my study animals!

HOW MANY POLECATS?

The number of polecats living in an area – the population density – is primarily determined by the abundance and diversity of available prey, which influences the size of home range that each polecat needs to occupy in order to support itself year-round. In prey-poor areas, such as overgrazed uplands with little cover and few rabbits, each polecat needs a large home range (> 300 hectares) so population densities are low; in prey-rich areas, such as lowland sandy farmland with many rabbits, home ranges tend to be smaller (often < 100 hectares) so population densities are higher. So average home range sizes may be a useful guide to population density, although we have to remember that male and female home ranges often overlap and males tend to occupy bigger ranges than females, so the link between home range size and population density is not quite direct; furthermore, different studies sometimes use different methods to measure home range area, which may undermine direct comparisons.

Because male polecats have bigger bodies than females (so they need more food) and because of the reproductive advantages of having a home range that overlaps with those of one or more females, males tend to have bigger home ranges than do females in the same area. For example, in Philip Blandford's 1980s study in mid Wales male polecats occupied average home ranges of 119 hectares and females occupied 64 hectares; in my 1990s VWT study in the English West Midlands, the figures were 212 hectares for males and 125 hectares for females; and in Lauren Harrington's 2000s study in Oxfordshire it was 88 hectares for males and 71 hectares for females. With a system of overlapping home ranges that each occupied, on average, a minimum of well over half a square kilometre one can see that population densities, even in relatively rich lowland farmland habitat, are unlikely to be high.

While I was working on polecats for the VWT in the 1990s I conceived a cunning plan that might enable me to achieve two very different aims: to gather useful information on how polecat numbers varied from place to place across their expanding British range; and to enable naturalists to enjoy close encounters with live wild polecats that they would never have otherwise. I devised a live-trapping system based on kilometre squares of the Ordnance Survey's national grid and advertised for volunteers who would be willing to help set and then check 16 traps over seven consecutive nights between October and March in a square close to their homes; this trapping period was chosen because polecat populations are relatively high and stable over the winter period, between the hurly-burly of juvenile dispersal in late summer and the testosterone-fuelled wanderings of rutting males in the spring.

I was overwhelmed by the positive response from naturalists all over Wales and England, who kindly signed up for the survey, secured landowner permission and rearranged their lives so as to check the traps early each morning after we had set them together. On the trap-setting day I provided training and written guidance on 'what to do if you catch something', and supplied a set of kit to enable the volunteers to mark, weigh and release any polecats without getting bitten; I also tried to lower expectations by warning that polecats are thin on the ground so we cannot expect to catch them everywhere; I lost count of the times I heard myself saying 'well, negative data are important too'. Dai Jermyn of the VWT played a key part in the later stages of this work. The whole project was conducted under licences issued by the government agencies that were then called the Countryside Council for Wales and English Nature.

Over five consecutive winters in the mid 1990s about 150 volunteers completed trapping sessions in 136 kilometre squares; most were spread across Wales and the English Midlands, but six were up in Cumbria where a reintroduced polecat population was established. Because each polecat trapped was given a visible short-term mark (using coloured stock-marker spray applied through the mesh of the trap before each animal was released), it was possible to identify how many individuals were caught in each square over the seven nights of trapping: in 56.1 per cent of kilometre squares where polecats were caught only one individual was recorded (not surprising given the low population density suggested by home range size information); exceptionally, in 10.6 per cent of polecat-positive squares, more than four individuals were recorded (suggesting that the trapping area coincided with the overlap of several home ranges). So this gives us some indication of the minimum number of polecats per kilometre square where they were recorded as present: overall the average number of individuals recorded in positive kilometre squares was 1.86. However, if we take account of the negative kilometre squares (in which no polecats were caught) it brings the average down to 0.9 polecats per kilometre square. This is a more realistic estimate of the average winter population density of polecats on farmland in England and Wales.

Two studies in Britain have revealed unusually high numbers of polecats at a site, and these probably arose because of their exceptionally high rabbit populations that rarely occur elsewhere: Kate Williamson's live-trapping study on coastal sand dunes in southern Snowdonia recorded up to eleven resident polecats in an area of one square kilometre; and one of the VWT's one kilometre square study sites near Ledbury in Herefordshire, which I live-trapped monthly over one winter, recorded ten polecats present in October/November, though numbers recorded as present fell steadily for unknown reasons to five in December and just one in February.

Another factor that still influences the local and national numbers of polecats is the geographical pattern of population recovery in Britain: as the population expands into new areas, not surprisingly, population densities are initially low and take some time to build up; this may be partly because there is less competition for space towards the advancing front of the species' range, so polecats can occupy larger home ranges there; also the polecats themselves may be more patchily distributed in the newly recolonised fringe areas when compared with the densely packed western core of the species' range. Some of these differences are reflected in the results of the VWT's 1990s live-trapping study, which showed that polecats were more likely to be recorded in trapping squares in the core of the range (most of Wales and the English border counties of Cheshire, Shropshire and Herefordshire) than towards the fringes in the English Midlands, where the proportion of negative squares was higher. Also, there were slight differences in the average number of individuals recorded per square, with 1.01 polecats per kilometre square in the core and 0.69 per square at the fringe.

These two average population density figures were used by the VWT to compute simple polecat population estimates for the whole occupied area of Britain: in 1997 there were estimated to be 38,381 polecats; and, following further range expansion, by 2006 the estimate had increased to 46,784. This figure is likely to grow steadily if the polecat is able to continue the current recolonisation of its former range. If we allow the polecat to make a full recovery so that it eventually reoccupies all suitable habitat in Britain, and so long as our managed landscapes provide an adequate density and diversity of uncontaminated prey, it could one day exceed the population of 110,055 estimated to exist here in Mesolithic times before our Neolithic ancestors began clearing the wildwood (the Mesolithic population estimate is derived from modern data on polecat abundance in Białowieza Forest in eastern Poland – our closest surviving approximation to the ancient wildwood). Why might polecat numbers eventually exceed the Mesolithic population estimate? Because polecats seem to thrive in Britain's more diverse modern landscapes; because we have helpfully introduced new sources of polecat food such as rabbits and rats; and because we have conveniently removed other predators such as wolves and lynx that would otherwise compete for polecat prey and might limit polecat numbers in other ways.

SOCIAL LIFE

Territoriality
Adult polecats live mainly solitary lives, apart from when they get together in the spring mating season to make new polecats, and in summer when breeding females rear their litters, with each one occupying a patch of ground that is known as a home range or territory (these terms have slightly different meanings, but are essentially much the same and refer to the area of land occupied and/or defended by a resident adult polecat). By this means the population spaces itself out in relation to the available resources. Like most of the smaller mustelids, the polecat's spacing system is based on intra-sexual territoriality, which is scientist-speak for individuals tolerating only a territory overlap with those of the opposite gender; so it is normal for male and female territories to overlap to some degree, and unusual for males to overlap with males and females with females.

How strictly the polecat conforms to this territory pattern is questionable, for some have suggested that its territoriality may be more weakly developed than in other small mustelids; notably polecats seem much less inclined to mark their territories with scats in the way that other carnivores do, unless we humans are simply less skilled at finding polecat scats compared with otter spraints, badger dung pits and fox scats? We still have much to learn about how polecats maintain their spacing system and the role that scent-marking might play.

One of my lucky encounters with polecats in the west of England suggests that under certain circumstances there is territorial flexibility, even between animals of the same gender. While radio-tracking two unrelated males occupying neighbouring territories on Herefordshire farmland in winter 1994, one morning I was surprised to find both radio signals coming from the same rat-infested farmyard where their territories joined. On 11 of the following 13 days I recorded both animals together in the same farmyard and recorded 19 simultaneous locations, which enabled me to estimate how far apart they were: on six occasions the males were more than 50 metres apart, hunting or resting in different parts of the farmyard, but on 13 occasions they were within 15 metres so must have been aware of each other's presence; and on two memorable occasions they were found within the same barn sleeping only two metres apart in the same small stack of hay bales. This indicates to me that, where there is an unusual surplus of polecat prey (the farmyard in question supported a very high rat population), neighbouring territory-holders of the same gender may tolerate each other's presence to the extent that both are able to exploit such prey richness without the usual aggression. The fact that both males chose to rest for the day in the same stack of hay suggests familiarity and mutual acceptance, and their combined use of the farmyard over several days implies a willingness to share resources in what was truly an area of territory overlap.

Communication

In contrast with social mammals such as Canids (the dog family), which have expressive lips, eyebrows and ears controlled by many facial muscles to create the snarling and cowering involved in dominance and submission, the polecat has an expressionless face that gives nothing away. Living mainly solitary lives, polecats simply have no need for the variety of facial signals used in close-quarters communication. However, they do communicate in other ways based mainly on scent.

For small carnivores like the polecat, which spend most of their lives pottering about quietly (so as not to disturb their prey) on their own in the dark, often in dense cover, olfactory (scent-based) communication is a brilliant invention, and the mustelid family has rather built its reputation on it! All mustelids use a cunning system of slow-release, whiffy chemical messages to maintain their territories, deter intruders and to find mates. Each end of a polecat has a crucial part to play, with the anal glands and bladder producing different types of scent and the nose and brain detecting and interpreting the scented messages left by others. As well as the stinky, highly volatile component that is designed to achieve an instant air-borne deterrent effect (giving the polecat its unfortunate smelly reputation), the paired, pea-sized anal scent glands also produce an oily, scented paste that coats the faeces and is also used to mark objects when a polecat 'sets scent' by pressing or rubbing its anal region onto a stone or log; this paste is the source of slow-release scent used by polecats to exchange information. Like other carnivores polecats have other scent glands in the skin on the underside of their bodies, especially on the throat, which they use to leave scent by rubbing against solid objects. As well as passing information between different polecats, scent-marking may serve to warn other small carnivores to avoid an area where a polecat is active. Polecats probably also use their urine for communication between individuals.

We don't know exactly how all this scent-based communication works specifically in relation to polecats; but in other carnivores we believe that scats, scent marks and urine provide information on individual identity, including gender, age, dominance and reproductive state. Chemical analyses, by Zhang and colleagues at Indiana University, of the urine and anal gland secretions of domestic ferrets give us insights into the types of information polecats can derive from each careful sniff: ferret urine was found to contain 30 volatile compounds that showed significant differences between both genders and individuals; and anal gland secretions contained several other different volatile compounds, suggesting that urine and anal scent might be used to convey different messages, although in either case the two products should enable a polecat to determine the gender and individual identity of another polecat, and so to discriminate between friend, foe and potential mate.

Further insights are provided in a study, by Rachel Berzins and Remi Helder of the University of Angers, of domestic ferret reactions to three different types of ferret odour from members of the opposite sex – urine, anal secretions and body odour – with special reference to their possible roles in mate choice: they found that female ferrets were not interested in male body odour, yet males were quite interested in female BO; males were more interested than females in the urine odours of the opposite sex; and both genders were equally interested in the anal scent of the opposite sex and were able to discriminate between familiar and unfamiliar anal scents. The authors concluded that this might influence each female's choices of which males to engage in olfactory communication with, for example by counter-marking a male's anal scent mark with one of her own (like an encouraging reply to a saucy text or email), with a preference being shown for familiar males over unfamiliar ones.

Adult polecats are silent for most of their lives, but they are capable of making a wide variety of sounds that must play some part in close-quarters communication with other polecats during both friendly and aggressive encounters or during courtship; they also make some sounds that help to warn or deter other animals (including humans) that might threaten them.

Polecat noises have been described in many ways by different authors: adults may respond to threats by hissing, chattering, chirring, yelping or screaming; they also make gentler chattering, chuntering and clucking sounds in more relaxed situations (these will be familiar to ferret-keepers); similar sounds are made by young polecats during their play. The only noise I have heard from a wild polecat is a sudden, sharp 'chack' sound made by a nervous animal waiting in a cage trap just before I released it; the sound was combined with a strong lunging movement in my direction with the mouth partly open, which served to warn me to be very careful! This sort of behaviour is known as a 'defensive threat'.

The polecat's social calendar

Like most mammals, the polecat's activity through the year is largely shaped by the fluctuating influences of hormones and prey availability, and by the demands of juveniles. Polecats don't hibernate, but their level of activity in mid winter is lower than at other times of the year; these variations in activity are typically reflected in the changing abundance of polecat road casualties. The chart below is a simple summary of what polecats of each gender are typically doing in each month of the year in Britain and how this is reflected in the pattern of road casualties that we might see.

Jan	Both genders relatively inactive so few road casualties; foraging includes visits to farmyards to prey on rats and mice; testes growing and males putting on weight especially around neck and shoulders.
Feb	Male activity increasing as testes approach full size, so slightly more road casualties; some mating activity towards end of month; males approaching peak bodyweight.
Mar	The main mating month, with males travelling furiously in search of receptive females; much fighting between males; peak month for adult male road casualties; foraging may focus on spawning amphibians on mild, wet nights.
Apr	Mating season continues; more male road casualties; most females start their pregnancies and choose their natal dens; both genders

	start to moult into their short, dark summer pelage (females use the moulted fur to line their breeding dens); both genders bear fresh scars on their necks from fighting and mating activity.
May	Most females give birth and stay close to their natal dens; males in poor body condition with flaccid testes and becoming less active as mating season ends, so fewer road casualties; moult completed so both genders in summer pelage by end of month.
Jun	A few more births; most females lactating and very busy catching food for their young, and may move litters to new dens; males relatively inactive with regressing testes and slim necks once more; female road casualties may outnumber those of males; adult females seen out foraging in daylight; juveniles may join mothers on foraging trips from middle of month.
Jul	Polecat families seen out and about; adult females continue to support their growing offspring and teach them how to forage independently; juvenile road casualties start to appear.
Aug	More juvenile road casualties as young become independent and dispersal starts towards end of month; adult females typically in poor condition and lighter in weight than their offspring.
Sep	Main month for juvenile dispersal and territory establishment, so big peak in juvenile road casualties; adult females start to recover body condition.
Oct	Still many road casualties as post-dispersal population is at its annual peak; both genders foraging busily to build body condition before winter.
Nov	Levels of activity decline in both genders; foraging may include visits to farmyards to catch rodents that move in from the fields post-harvest.
Dec	A quiet month, with lowest numbers of road casualties; much foraging in farmyards to exploit concentrations of commensal rodents; testis growth starts in response to shortening day-length.

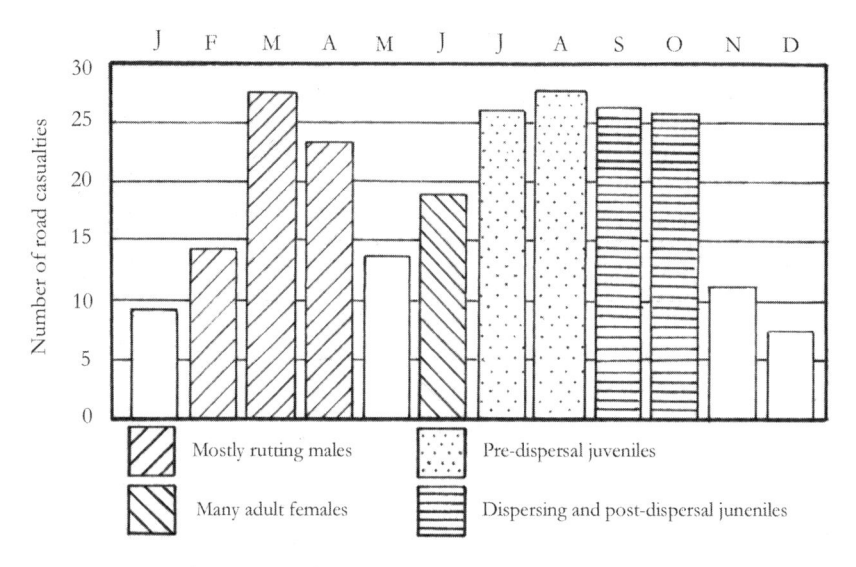

The pattern of polecat road casualties over a typical year, showing those sectors of the population that tend to dominate the figures in particular months.

Mating and pregnancy

For male polecats the spring mating season is a hectic, hormone-fuelled hunt for females on heat; for females it is a case of avoiding serious injury at the hands – or teeth, to be accurate – of the much stronger males, whilst attempting to exert some choice over which male or males might father their kits. Both genders face tough physical challenges: pairs of males frequently fight when competing for access to a female in oestrus, with much biting around the sides of the neck as each male grips, shoves and rolls to gain the upper hand; and females have to endure the painful mustelid mating process involving a male gripping her nape with his canine teeth while he drags her about, manhandles (or mantooths?) her into position and restrains her during copulation, which may last for an hour. There is a physiological logic to this brutality for, whilst female polecats come into oestrus as a consequence of their own hormonal activity linked to changing day-length, ovulation has to be induced by copulation involving more than a hint of male violence and perhaps a whiff of pheromones.

Induced ovulation is common in solitary mammals living at low population densities; by contrast social mammals like we humans tend to be spontaneous ovulators, in which the ovaries release eggs according to an oestrus cycle whether or not mating has occurred. The obvious advantage of ovulation induced by copulation is that it removes the element of chance involved in sperm and eggs meeting at the right time and place, and thereby it avoids the wastage of valuable eggs that might otherwise be released when there are no males nearby to fertilise them.

The timing of the polecat mating season is controlled by photoperiod: changes in the relative durations of daylight and darkness trigger hormonal activity in the pituitary gland, which in turn influences the production of hormones that control fertility. Although early spring is the peak polecat mating period in Britain, for the males physical changes begin in mid winter, probably at the approach of the shortest day at the winter solstice detected by the pituitary gland, which triggers testis growth and associated hormone-driven changes in male musculature and elevated levels of activity and aggression. In contrast the female polecat's pituitary gland activity seems to be triggered by increasing day-length, so that she comes into oestrus in early spring and remains in this state until either she is mated or day-length shortens in late summer, leading to hormonal changes via the pituitary. Unmated females may remain in oestrus from late February through to the end of August, and while in this condition the vulva is very swollen and obvious as a bald, bulbous area of skin beneath the tail and in front of the anus (ferret-keepers used to believe that unmated females would die because of the physiological strain and risk of infection arising from prolonged oestrus).

In males the first changes are apparent in December, when the previously tiny or invisible (in first-winter males) testes begin to swell; by February they are very obvious as taut and furry paired sacs beneath the tail, and sperm production is under way; also by February males have developed greater muscle mass in the neck and shoulders to equip them for fighting other males and restraining females; and males range more widely in search of local females, reflected in a steep increase in male road casualties apparent from January to March; March is also the month when male polecats reach their peak body weight, with accumulated muscle and fat designed to power and fuel them through the mating season.

Ken Walton's scrutiny of polecat testes shows that sperm are abundant from mid February through to mid May, with a sparse presence of sperm continuing into June; so males remain capable of inseminating females over at least four months if any remain in oestrus for that long.

Although the period when both sexes are potentially fertile runs from late February to June, most polecat matings occur early on in this period for the following reasons: firstly a female's oestrus ends with ovulation, conception and her subsequent pregnancy, so there is pressure on fertile males to find and mate with any receptive females as early as possible because, if other males are active in the area, there will soon be no oestrus females left; secondly, the earlier polecats kits are born – and provided prey are suitably abundant for their mother to catch – the longer they have to grow in size and confidence before dispersing to establish their own territories in the autumn; members of late-born litters probably fail to compete successfully for vacant territories because, being younger, they are smaller and weaker than their rivals. So most polecat mating activity occurs between late February and early April, with March the most hectic month of all. If the spring surge in polecat road casualties – always heavily dominated by rutting males – is a reliable proxy for mating activity, then week-by-week records from the VWT's polecat survey covering 2014 and 2015 suggest that the passionate peak in amorous 'polecat action' occurs in the third week of March in Britain. Indeed hormone-fuelled male polecats are so keen to spread their genes that they are easily attracted by the scent of a domestic ferret in oestrus, with reports each spring of attempted or actual break-ins at ferret hutches in back gardens.

Because such things are so difficult to study in wild, free-living populations, we know very little about what strategies are adopted by male polecats of different ages and sizes during the mating season, and what choice, if any, females have over which males mate with them. However, Trevor Poole made observations of reproductive behaviour in captive polecats: he found that receptive females elicited behaviour in males that led directly to copulation, while unreceptive females simply led to males trying harder by changing their behaviour (so no change there then!). Poole also noted the influence of male experience: inexperienced males simply grabbed an oestrus female and tried to mate with her, usually failing because they did not seize the nape in the way that experienced males did; so the nape grip has to be learnt before a male can achieve a successful mating.

We can also get some ideas about likely polecat mating strategies from studies of other mustelids. A study of stoat movements in Sweden by Mikael Sandell suggests that males fall into three mate-searching categories depending upon age and social status: 'stayers', 'roamers' and 'transients'; with bigger, older males ranging more widely and mating more females then their younger competitors, which bide their time until they have the bulk and confidence to compete successfully at the highest level in future years. Studying kit paternity among free-living American mink in the Thames valley, Nobby Yamaguchi found that females were able to 'mix and match' the sperm of their different partners during the promiscuous mating season so as to produce litters with multiple paternity, perhaps maximising the later contributions of males with the greatest staying power (although this system may only have been possible because of the mink's short delayed implantation of embryos, which is not available to polecats).

Thus, in the polecat mating system, which is probably just as promiscuous as that of stoats and mink, it seems likely that the biggest, strongest and most experienced males travel widely, compete successfully and, thereby, mate with several different females; while, like the young Swedish stoats, inexperienced yearling male polecats may try their luck with one or two neighbouring females but otherwise stay put and wait until their second mating season before mixing it with the big boys.

After the rigours of the mating season many males carry fresh fighting scars on the sides of their necks, matched by the puncture wounds that they have inflicted on the females' napes. From April onwards males lose weight and their testes become flaccid and shrink gradually, while pregnant females grow plump and choose their natal dens with care; both sexes become much less active so the number of road casualties drops to an early summer low in May. There is no hint of pair bonding as found in some mammals; this is unsurprising because each female polecat may have been mated by more than one male, so why would any male choose to invest effort in rearing young if he cannot be sure he is their father? So the tough job of rearing polecat kits falls entirely to the females. This task so drains their energy reserves that, by the end of the summer, mother polecats typically appear thin and exhausted; so there is no possibility of a female rearing more than one litter in a season. In exceptional circumstances, such as when her litter dies early on, a female may come into oestrus a second time; but if this occurs after June there may be no fertile males available to mate with her.

Unlike some other small mustelids, such as martens, mink and stoats, there is no delayed implantation in polecats. So, soon after mating and conception, the embryos implant and develop through a gestation of usually 42 days, though it may range between 40 and 44. As her pregnancy advances through its final stages the female moults fur from her belly, so that her growing teats (6 – 10 in number) are easy for her kits to find and so she has some soft, insulating material with which to line the natal den, as the site where she gives birth and starts to rear her kits is known. In fact the spring moult of her entire coat, which starts in April, is conveniently timed to provide lots of spare fur in time for the kits to snuggle amongst it in the natal den.

The ideal natal den should possess the following characteristics in order to give a mother polecat the best chance of rearing her litter successfully: it should be a secure, snug, dry, draught-free structure that provides insulation and protection from weather, with an entrance hole small enough to exclude potential predators; its location should be away from the risk of flooding and other environmental hazards; and it should be located close enough to good foraging habitat and a variety of suitable prey populations so that the mother does not have to travel far nor be away hunting for long periods when the young are vulnerable.

Because there have been so few studies of polecats in Britain during the breeding season we know little about the full range of natal den sites used. However, thanks to reports from members of the public, we do know that some polecat litters are born in or under outhouses, garden sheds, garages and garden decking, and occasionally even within houses, under floorboards or in lofts, for example; and farmers have reported polecat litters associated with stacks of hay and straw in farmyards and cavities within or beneath barns. But this is a biased sample because it reflects mainly the observations made where people spend most of their time, and so it reveals only the types of natal den most likely to be noticed, such as those close to human habitation. A radio-tracking study of pregnant polecats would doubtless reveal a different range of natal dens in more cryptic locations such as rabbit burrows, rocky crevices and among tree roots.

Birth and juvenile development

The number of polecat kits in a litter may range from 2 to 12, but the norm is 5–10, with some early mortality so that by weaning time most litters number seven or less. The number of kits surviving to weaning is determined mainly by the foraging skills of their mother and the abundance of suitable prey in her home range: in lean years when rabbit and vole populations are low there may be high pre-weaning mortality, with smaller litters emerging from the den as a consequence.

The timing of births in the wild is difficult to establish, but Ken Walton made some calculations based upon the date when juveniles were first observed outside of natal dens, which was late July and August in his sample of mainly Welsh polecat records from the 1960s. On this basis, and estimating that emergent juveniles were about 60 days old, he judged that the first births were at the end of May, with most occurring in June; this would suggest that the peak mating period was in April. Thirty to fifty years later and informed by a very large VWT sample of both Welsh and English records from the 1990s through to the 2010s my perception is of a significantly earlier birth date: heavily pregnant females were recorded from late April; lactating female road casualties occurred from 12 May; a live juvenile was recovered on 20 May (presumably having emerged from a den following the death of its mother); the first juvenile road casualty was on 3 June; mother polecats were observed carrying kits from one den to another as early as 10 May (but mostly in early June); and juveniles were commonly reported out of dens with their mothers from mid June through July. Based on these observations the peak period for polecat births must be in early May, which, after a six-week gestation, concurs with mid to late March being the peak period for matings (as suggested above by the timing of the peak in rutting male road casualties). However, a few births undoubtedly occur later than May, with observations of quite young litters reported occasionally from August and even September; these indicate that a small number of births must occur in June or July.

Young polecats are born weighing 9–10 grams with their eyelids and ears closed and their bodies thinly covered with fine, silver fur. Early on the kits are wholly dependent upon their mother for food, warmth and sanitation services (the mother licks her kits' genitals and anuses to stimulate their bladders and bowels). Much of what we know about how young polecats develop comes from the observations of ferret-breeders, for the developmental stages of the wild and domestic forms are much the same; most of the timings in the table below are taken from James McKay's book *Ferret Breeding*.

Kit age	Developmental stage
14–18 days	Deciduous teeth erupt
2–3 weeks	Start to eat solid food – still taking milk
3–4 weeks	Silvery fur replaced by darker grey-brown, soft, woolly coat with off-white chins, muzzles and ear tips
32–33 days	Ears open
30–36 days	Eyes open
5 weeks	Kits start to play and explore inside the natal den
5–6 weeks	Fur dominated by very dark guard hairs over grey-brown undercoat, so kits appear blackish all over with off-white chins, muzzles and ear tips
6 weeks	Weaning complete – eating only solid food
47–52 days	Adult canine teeth erupt
9 weeks	Off-white fur patches develop between eyes and ears, which then may join across forehead and elongate down towards jaw angle to define the 'mask'; appear like small adults and now accompany mother away from the den

Mother polecats suckle their young until they are weaned at about six weeks of age; and from about three weeks onwards mothers bring fresh prey back to the natal den to start the weaning process. At this stage it is crucial that suitable prey is available nearby and it is a huge help if wild rabbits are present and breeding within a mother polecat's home range, because every bunny litter represents a conveniently portable takeaway feast to carry back to the natal den (adult rabbits present more of a challenge to carry home). A series of 37 photographs taken by Chris Turner on 18 June 2014 and passed to the VWT record such a predation event on the edge of his garden on the Welsh border one sunny morning around breakfast time: over a period of 45 minutes an adult female polecat found and excavated a rabbit breeding 'stop' and removed the kittens one by one and carried them away out of the garden, presumably to feed her own kits in a den not very far away.

The heavy energetic demands of lactation and the extra foraging time required to provide increasing quantities of prey means that mid summer is a very tough time for mother polecats: they tend to be active both by day and night in order to catch sufficient food, and they range widely and busily throughout their home ranges in order to exploit all sources of prey; consequently June tends to be the peak month for adult female road casualties (and the only month of the year when more female polecats are killed on the roads than males). Because adult females in June are either still lactating or have weaned but still-dependent young, this is also the peak month for orphan polecats, a few of which are fortunate enough to be recovered and reared by wildlife rescue centres and the RSPCA.

June to August is the period when polecat families comprising mothers and young are most likely to be seen out and about in daylight, and the first evidence of such families is mother polecats seen carrying their kits one by one by the scruff of the neck from one den to another; usually this is reported in the first half of June, but occasionally as early as mid May. The reasons for this urgent house-moving are not clear, but may be to do with a build-up of parasites or smelly prey remains and faeces in the original den; or the den may have become unsafe or unsuitable in some other way, such as depletion of a local prey source. Up to mid June the kits normally stay close to the den, but once they are mobile and strong enough the mother will encourage them to follow her on foraging trips and visits to different dens, with frequent reports of families seen moving together in daylight in late June and July. Reports often relate to polecat families seen on roads during daylight, sometimes with fatal consequences.

One such report (fortunately with no sad ending) was described to me by Simon Edwards, who encountered a mother polecat and six or seven well-grown young while he was driving on a minor road on Swallowcliffe Down in Wiltshire at 2.30 p.m. on 20 June 2006. He spotted what looked like a mobile, furry, black and tan lump on the edge of the tarmac a few tens of metres ahead of his vehicle. As he approached the swarming mass he stopped his car and took photographs through the windscreen: these reveal a dense group of at least seven polecats (it's very hard to count them accurately because they are so intertwined) loitering by the long grass of the verge; in each image the mother is always identifiable because she is 'on guard', keeping a sharp eye on the vehicle as she shepherds her young off the road and into the grass. This must have been a reasonably early litter because, well before the end of June, the young polecats were nearly as big as their mother; and to rear so many to that size suggests she had access to some good prey populations within her home range.

Juvenile dispersal

In August young polecats become progressively less dependent upon their exhausted mothers as they learn to forage for themselves within her territory. This growing independence within the safety of their mother's domain is a prelude to dispersal, the instinctive process involving young polecats setting off in search of their own territories at the end of the summer. It has much in common with the time when human teenagers head off to college and university, and the sighs of parental (strictly maternal in the polecat's case) relief are probably just as loud!

In polecats juvenile dispersal mainly occurs in September, with youngsters leaving their natal ranges to search for a vacant patch in which to settle and establish a territory. It is a very challenging time for young polecats, which may travel considerable distances through unfamiliar landscapes, facing a range of scary new hazards, including aggressive encounters as they pass through territories occupied by other polecats. The lucky ones quickly find and settle in a territory vacated following the death of another polecat over the preceding year, or establish a new territory in an area of countryside unoccupied at the fringe of the species' distribution. The less fortunate may have to adopt a risky, nomadic lifestyle for weeks before they either settle or die. Inevitably there is high mortality, with juveniles dominating the road casualty figures for September and October.

Juvenile dispersal plays an important part in the spacing and genetic mixing of polecat populations; it also facilitates a population's expansion into new areas, so is a major driver of the polecat's current recolonisation of its former range in Britain. Considering its significance it is a pity, though not surprising, that we know so little about how dispersal operates in polecats, nor in most other British carnivores for that matter. Compared with bird ringing schemes, which yield valuable data on patterns of dispersal and migration for many species, scarce carnivores are too inaccessible and have too few people interested in them for us to gather such information.

Lifespan
The key to a long and happy life for a polecat is to secure a prey-rich home range that contains no busy roads, no traps, and no farmyards laced with rodenticides. With all these boxes ticked, and barring any diseases or other premature fatal misfortune, a polecat may easily live for four or five years in the wild (exceptionally polecats have been recorded up to eight years old in the wild, and even older in captivity). This typical maximum lifespan masks the huge variation within the population, with reckless young males suffering especially high mortality: Ken Walton calculated their life expectancy at birth as just 8.1 months; and in Switzerland Darius Weber estimated that 80 per cent of male polecats die in their first year. This sounds both tough and wasteful, but it is the standard mechanism by which populations of small carnivores regulate their numbers in relation to the food available; without it we would be wading knee-deep through a pungent sea of starving polecats. Essentially, if a young polecat cannot find a suitable home range in its first autumn its future is very bleak indeed.

TROPHIC MATTERS
(FOOD AND FORAGING)

Scats tell all

Dietary studies are crucial to an understanding of carnivores' ecology – they give us insights into how the animals hunt, what habitats they forage in and when, and the extent to which they compete with other predators. This explains why so many carnivore biologists – who typically struggle to observe their study animals out foraging – are obsessed with finding droppings (known as scats) and identifying their contents (surely the true origin of the phrase 'going through the motions'?), and why a researcher friend of mine once had a small but heartfelt sign above his desk that quietly squealed 'It may be just sh*t to you, but it's my bread and butter!'

Polecats are extra awkward because, unlike foxes, badgers, otters and mink, for example, they don't leave their scats in obvious places for biologists to find easily; nor are polecat scats distinctive enough to separate them easily from those of other animals such as mink and feral ferrets. This means that polecat diet studies have relied mainly on analyses of stomach contents of animals killed in traps or by vehicles, or of scats collected from the dens of radio-tagged polecats where researchers have little doubt about which animal produced them. For this reason there have been rather few studies of the polecat's diet, except in those countries where polecats have been trapped and killed for their fur (leading to easy access to stomachs, which nevertheless tend to be empty because of the time the animals spend held in traps before they die).

Ken Walton's was the first scientific study of polecat diet in Britain: he identified the stomach contents of 38 animals killed by vehicles or in traps during the mid 1960s, when polecats were still mainly confined to Wales and rabbits were still scarce following the serious effects on rabbit numbers of *Myxomatosis*; so his findings reflect those particular constraints. What emerged was a rather broad diet comprising mammals (35.1 per cent of prey items), birds (14.0 per cent), amphibians and reptiles (26.3 per cent) and invertebrates (24.6 per cent), with a few miscellaneous items and plant material probably ingested accidentally. The mammal component was made up of lagomorphs (rabbits and hares, with the former almost certainly dominating because polecats are unlikely to catch hares so easily), water vole, field vole, wood mouse and hedgehog (the contributions of each were not provided); no species or groups were specified in the bird component; the amphibians and reptiles comprised just common frog and common lizard (with the former prevalent in the diet), although snakes may also be taken occasionally; and the invertebrates included beetles, bees, moth and fly larvae, spider, slugs, snails and earthworms, some of which were probably either ingested as stomach contents of larger prey or were associated with carrion.

During his mid-1980s radio-tracking study of polecats in the hills of mid Wales, Philip Blandford searched the dens of his study animals and managed to gather 558 polecat scats. In those he identified 754 prey items within 21 categories and comprising at least 30 species of mainly vertebrate prey. He presented dietary information in various ways, including as 'corrected percentage bulk', which is believed to reflect most closely the quantitative importance in the diet of each prey item (see table opposite). Note that invertebrates are included in the table with a zero value because they normally occurred only as insignificant trace items possibly ingested by chance; one study animal, however, appeared to take invertebrates deliberately, with 14 occurrences in 23 scats, including three scats composed mainly of a mix of earthworms and adult beetles. Among the amphibians it was not easy to identify the species involved, but the majority of remains were thought to be of frogs and toads rather than newts.

Because it is difficult to separate the remains of rabbits and hares in scats, these are lumped in the table as 'lagomorphs', but it is highly likely that all involved rabbits because much of Blandford's radio-tagged polecats' foraging behaviour was focused on areas of rabbit activity and also because polecats are not likely to catch many hares. If this assumption is correct, rabbits were by far the most important dietary item in this mid-Wales study, suggesting that this species had become more abundant since Ken Walton's earlier study in the post-*Myxomatosis* era of rabbit scarcity.

In the 1990s a further study of polecat diet, focusing on England for the very first time, was completed by National Museums Scotland (NMS) and The Vincent Wildlife Trust (summarised in the table on page 82). Stomach contents were identified from 83 road casualty polecats across eleven counties in the English Midlands (63 per cent of stomachs came from just

Prey type	Corrected % bulk
Invertebrates	0.0
Amphibians	3.9
Anseriforme birds (ducks)	1.1
Galliforme birds (game and poultry)	5.3
Gruiforme birds (e.g. rails and coots)	1.3
Charadriiforme birds (waders)	1.8
Gulls	0.2
Columbiforme birds (pigeons)	1.9
Passeriforme birds (perching birds)	1.9
Unidentified birds	1.7
Hedgehog	0.3
Shrews	0.3
Mole	0.2
Bank vole	4.5
Field vole	2.5
Wood mouse	6.3
House mouse	0.5
Rat	1.5
Squirrel	1.0
Lagomorphs (rabbit and hare)	63.2
Unidentified mammals	0.8

The diet of polecats in mid Wales during the 1980s, shown as the corrected percentage bulk of identifiable remains in scats (after Blandford, 1986).

three counties: Shropshire, Herefordshire and Worcestershire); and in this study account was taken of the weight of different prey items present in stomachs, so that the proportions of different foods more closely reflected their actual contribution to the diet (in the absence of this adjustment the significance of tiny items such as invertebrates may be exaggerated, while that of larger prey such as rabbit is underplayed).

Following the two earlier studies of Welsh polecats, the trend of an increasing contribution of rabbits to the polecat's diet continues (by the 1990s rabbit populations had substantially recovered from the effects of *Myxomatosis*): rabbit comprised 85 per cent of the weight of identifiable

Prey type	% weight	% stomachs
Rabbit	85.4	72.3
Polecat	0.4	1.2
Common rat	1.8	2.4
Bat	0.2	1.2
Field vole	1.7	2.4
Bank vole	0.3	1.2
Wood mouse	1.0	3.6
Unidentified small mammal	0.01	1.2
Total Mammals	90.7	
Columbiforme birds (pigeons)	2.4	3.6
Passeriforme birds (perching birds)	0.03	2.4
Charadriiforme birds (waders)	0.03	1.2
Unidentified birds	0.06	2.4
Total Birds	3.0	
Amphibians	4.6	8.4
Fish	0.01	1.2
Earthworms	1.8	2.4

The diet of polecats in the English Midlands during the 1990s, shown as the percentage weight of identifiable remains in stomachs and the percentage of stomachs in which those identifiable remains occurred (after Birks and Kitchener, 1999).

prey and occurred in 72 per cent of stomachs; indeed 67.5 per cent of English polecat stomachs contained nothing but rabbit remains. Inevitably other prey items made only minor contributions, with amphibians ranking as the second most important group at 4.6 per cent of prey weight and 8.4 per cent of stomachs (only common frogs and common toads were recorded).

Foraging for rabbits – underground operations

Rabbits are clearly a hugely important source of polecat food in Britain, but how does the polecat, not known for its speed over open ground, catch so many of them? The simple answer is that it does it underground using the element of surprise. The polecat is perfectly designed for exploring the maze of tunnels and chambers dug by rabbits: the long, low, sinuous body copes with every subterranean twist and turn, no matter how tight; stealthy tracking of scent trails guides it through total darkness towards the occupants, where the element of surprise combined with subterranean bunny panic invariably leads to a capture; sharp claws on the front feet and canine teeth embedded in flesh prevent escape, while the powerful neck and shoulders manipulate the victim so that the bite can be transferred to the neck area to puncture vital tubes and vessels to achieve a kill in true small mustelid style.

Where rabbits are common polecats spend a lot of their foraging time searching underground in rabbit burrows; they also use the burrows as convenient daytime resting sites. In the VWT's study in the west of England in the 1990s all the radio-tagged polecats made some use of rabbit burrows, and half of all radio fixes were from polecats underground in rabbit burrows. Of these 'burrow fixes' 32 per cent were from active polecats, mostly at night. Being underground and mainly nocturnal this foraging activity was impossible to observe, but occasionally I was close enough to hear the subterranean thumping of alarmed rabbits as they responded to 'my' radio-tagged polecat moving through the burrows in pursuit of its prey; and twice in daylight I saw rabbits bolting from burrows in response to a radio-tagged polecat foraging underground. Having killed a rabbit underground, a polecat would typically spend one to three days staying in the same burrow while it consumed the carcass in cosy, subterranean safety.

There was some individual variation in the level of use of rabbit burrows by radio-tagged polecats in the VWT study, though most spent more than half of their time in such sites either foraging or resting: two radio-tagged females spent more than 90 per cent of recorded time in rabbit burrows; one sub-adult spent so long (18 days) in the same set of burrows without moving much that I was concerned for her welfare so set traps to catch her – she had obviously fed extremely well on the resident rabbits because, when I finally caught her to check her condition, she was one of the heaviest female polecats ever recorded at just over one kilogram!

Gender variations in diet
Summaries of dietary information such as those presented above, derived from many animals over a wide area and from an extended period, tend

to mask interesting patterns of variation between individual polecats, between the two genders and the seasonal variations arising from differences in prey availability. For example, Blandford's 1980s study in mid Wales, involving collection of scats originating from known seasons, from radio-tagged polecats of known age and gender, enabled him to tease out some patterns. Seasonal variations in polecat diet tended to reflect the changing availability of their prey, so amphibians were consumed mostly in spring, lagomorphs (mainly rabbits) peaked in summer and small rodents were eaten most in the autumn and winter. Considering their fairly extreme sexual dimorphism in body size (on average males are nearly twice as heavy as females), which one might expect to be reflected in the selection of different prey, the year-round differences between male and female diets were very small: males tended to take more large birds (such as ducks, waders and gulls) and ate slightly more lagomorphs, squirrels, rats and wood mice than did the females; conversely females ate more voles and house mice than did the males. Similarly minor differences were found in the NMS/VWT study of English polecats in the 1990s: males were slightly more rabbit-obsessed than females (89 per cent compared with 71 per cent), and the females compensated by eating more birds (13 per cent compared with 1 per cent in the males' diet) and other mammals (12 per cent compared with 4 per cent) than the males.

Considering the quintessentially French interface between food and sex (strictly gender actually – *Moi?* Stereotyping *Les Francais? Non!*), polecats in the wetlands of western France revealed a most unexpected pattern of predation: Thierry Lodé's collection of polecat prey remains and stomach contents showed that, across a range of species from bank and meadow voles through rats to frogs and toads, males were caught and consumed disproportionately more than females in relation to their availability. This surprising selection of male prey over females is hard to explain beyond it being a consequence of the greater recklessness of males across many prey species, making them more prone to capture by predators. There is a certain evolutionary logic to this, of course, because we males are the more expendable gender in reproductive terms (this pattern of males dominating predator diets may be widespread, but the evidence is lacking because most people don't look for this sort of information in their studies). Pursuing his sexual (sorry, gender!) theme,

Lodé also looked for inter-gender differences in the diet of his polecats and, as in the studies above, found rather few overall. Where they did occur he noted that there was no tendency for the chunkier males to eat larger prey than the females did; he used this evidence to argue that trophic separation (i.e. the need to consume different prey so as to reduce or avoid competition between the two genders) is not the driver of sexual dimorphism in body size in polecats.

Rat control

Part of my work with the VWT involved a study of polecats' use of farmyards in winter, which led me to search for scats in the various nooks and crannies in sheds, barns and haystacks where my radio-tagged animals slept during the day. Haystacks were the favourite polecat resting site because the animals could squeeze through the gaps between the bales to find a dry, safe, sheltered bed inside the stack (some also used the narrow gaps between hay bales as a cunning way of reversing out of their radio collars, but that's another story). As each polecat slept I was able to pinpoint its location in the haystack by triangulating with my aerial and receiver from the muddy farmyard outside. This was important because each polecat resting site had a toilet area nearby within the stack where scats would accumulate and dry out in the damp-free conditions, and I was keen to get my hands on them to find out what the animals had been eating.

One Herefordshire farmer, Cedric Lawrence, was so interested in my study that he kindly saved any polecat toilets that he found in his haystack as he progressively removed the bales to feed his cattle over the winter. Thanks to him we gathered over 230 scats from two radio-tagged polecats that spent a lot of time in his rather rat-infested farmyard, and thanks to Chris Strachan (who kindly 'went through the motions'), we were able to tell Mr Lawrence exactly what his polecats were eating: not surprisingly common rats (65.5 per cent) were the dominant species in the diet, with other rodents comprising 16.6 per cent and rabbits just 13 per cent; birds made up 4.5 per cent and insects were a tiny 0.4 per cent. So this is an example of individual dietary preference not revealed by wide-scale studies, with two animals taking advantage of the winter concentration of rats in one farmyard; for the rest of the year these same polecats most likely preyed mainly upon rabbits in the surrounding fields and woods.

Mr Lawrence's farmyard was such a centre of winter polecat activity that I loitered there over many nights while trying to follow 'my' radio-tagged boys as they hunted rats and mice in and around his barns, cattle sheds and feed stores. The best nights were the cold, clear, calm ones, when sound travelled well through the frosty air. Standing stock still in the stiffening mud on such a night I could hear the squeaks, patters and rustlings from the large population of rats going about its bickering business of fraternising and feeding among the farmyard clutter. Against this background noise I frequently tuned my radio receiver to check whether the local polecat had finished his lie-in in the big hay stack just 20 metres from Mr Lawrence's bedroom window: variations in signal strength revealed that the polecat was on the move; a shiver of anticipation crept down my spine and I resisted the urge to stamp my feet against the cold, which might disturb him and his prey. How soon before he would enter the ratty zone less than 15 metres in front of me?

Despite the sudden arrival of painfully loud bleeping in my headphones that signalled the polecat's close proximity, I never saw him cross the farmyard beside me; but I could hear growing rodent hysteria as the polecat entered their world. The earlier ratty orchestra shifted in tone and volume as my midnight rambler started hunting in earnest: urgent squeals replaced the squeaks, and calm pattering and rustling turned to bumps, thumps and clattering as dozens of rats fought to find the quickest escape route; as the symphony built to its discordant crescendo a long drawn-out squeal told me that Mr Lawrence had one less rat to worry about; then shadowy shapes bolting across the frost-hardened mud reminded me that there were many more where that one came from.

A modern dietary generalist

Across its European range the polecat is viewed as a carnivorous generalist predator, which means that it is moderately good at catching a wide range of prey, from invertebrates and amphibians through small rodents and birds to larger prey such as rabbits. This generalist feeding behaviour is reflected in the diversity of prey types represented in the British studies described above, with the recent domination of rabbits in the polecat's diet occurring as a simple consequence of opportunism (in response to our unusual abundance of rabbits in many parts of Britain), rather than obligatory specialism. This means that if rabbits become scarce once again the polecat is capable of switching easily to alternative foods in the way that a specialist predator might not. For example, the otter is a specialist fish predator with superb adaptations that make it the leader in its field but which limit its ability to catch alternative prey; so the otter is an obligatory specialist that struggles to survive where and when fish are scarce. So the generalist polecat has the advantage of flexibility and 'prey-switching'; but it may run into trouble if faced with competition from too many specialist predators, or if alternative types of prey become scare for other reasons.

Polecats are almost exclusively carnivorous, with most occurrences of vegetable matter in their diets interpreted either as accidental ingestion or the stomach contents of their herbivorous prey. But in some circumstances polecats do eat fruit, as discovered by Chris Hall when he helped the VWT in its quest to find pine martens in North Wales in the 1990s: polecats dominated the captures when marten live-traps were baited with fresh meat, so the bait was switched to tinned fruit in order to increase the chances of catching the more frugivorous pine marten; surprisingly the local polecats continued to enter the traps and most of them ate all the fruit provided.

Variations in the availability of prey and competition from other predators influence the composition of the polecat's diet across its European range. For example, in many countries the rabbit is either scarce or absent, so other types of prey such as rodents or amphibians assume greater significance. Thierry Lodé reviewed 18 dietary studies across Europe and found only one outside Britain, in the Camargue in southern France, where rabbits made a comparable contribution (84 per cent); rodents dominated the diet in 10 studies and were of secondary importance in seven others; amphibians (mainly anurans – frogs and toads; newts are rarely recorded in polecat diets) came top in just three studies, but occupied second place in eight others. The combined polecat diet across those 18 European studies dating from the late 1930s to the mid 1990s reveals that rodents and amphibians together account for nearly 60 per cent of polecat prey, with lagomorphs comprising just 13 per cent and the remainder made up by other mammals, birds, carrion and invertebrates. Also, polecats on the Continent occasionally eat fish, reportedly trapping them in shallow water or taking fish rejected by fisherman; they have also been observed catching eels, which are vulnerable as adults when they move overland at night on their way back to the sea.

Just as in Britain where polecats feast on our abundant rabbits, elsewhere they are able to specialise on certain prey groups: for example in the well-wooded Jura Mountains of north-west Switzerland amphibians dominated the diet, with polecats switching to rodents and carrion in winter while the amphibians were hibernating; in parts of France and Belgium small rodents tended to dominate (both > 60 per cent of polecat diet). Even within a single country the varying patterns of land use shape polecat diets through their influence upon prey availability: in the near-pristine Białowieża Forest of eastern Poland amphibians made up 74 per cent of the diet, while in the more open agricultural landscapes of western Poland mammals (65 per cent) and birds (21 per cent) were dominant.

This last study, by Anna Malecha and Marcin Antczak in the Wielkopolska region of western Poland between 2006 and 2008, reveals just how broad the polecat's diet may be in a Central European agricultural landscape where a wide range of prey is available yet rabbits are absent: the authors identified at least nine species of small rodent (comprising 52 per cent of the diet) with the common vole (*Microtus arvalis*) the dominant species among a tasty mix of mice and other voles that included the occasional harvest mouse and water vole; unidentified mammals made up 14 per cent of the diet; infrequently consumed insectivores were represented by shrews, mole and hedgehog; domestic cat and deer were ingested as carrion; birds included mallard, domestic hen, magpie, blackbird, yellowhammer, siskin, grey partridge and woodpigeon; reptiles comprised lizards, grass snakes and slow worms; amphibians were frogs and toads; and the remainder was made up of minor occurrences of fruit, other plant matter, fish, invertebrates and a Natterer's bat.

Pre-historic anuran specialism?

Recent studies of polecats living in Białowieża Forest, which is on the Poland-Belarus border and is Europe's best surviving example of the once extensive 'wildwood', give us an insight into how the species probably behaved eight thousand years ago before we began clearing our forests for agriculture. Extrapolating back from the modern diet in Białowieża

POLECATS | TROPHIC MATTERS (FOOD AND FORAGING)

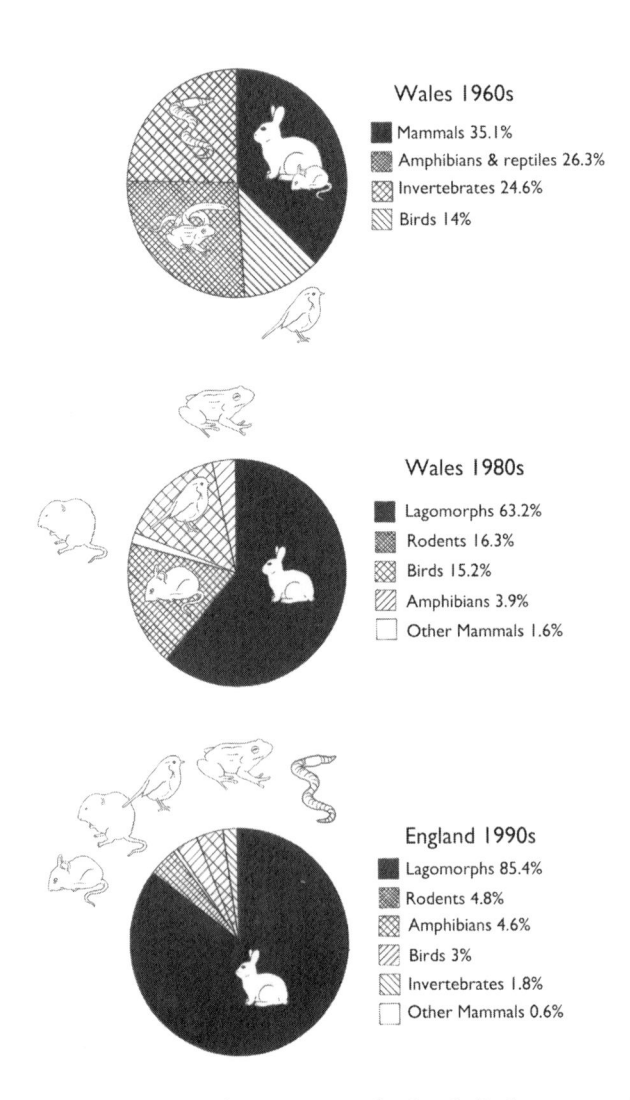

Wales 1960s
- Mammals 35.1%
- Amphibians & reptiles 26.3%
- Invertebrates 24.6%
- Birds 14%

Wales 1980s
- Lagomorphs 63.2%
- Rodents 16.3%
- Birds 15.2%
- Amphibians 3.9%
- Other Mammals 1.6%

England 1990s
- Lagomorphs 85.4%
- Rodents 4.8%
- Amphibians 4.6%
- Birds 3%
- Invertebrates 1.8%
- Other Mammals 0.6%

A summary of polecat diets from Britain, Poland and all of Europe, with the dominant prey category in each diet shown in black; this reveals how the proportion of lagomorphs in the diet of British polecats increased from the 1960s to the 1990s as rabbit populations recovered from the effects of Myxomatosis; and how broad is the diet of polecats across Europe as a whole.

POLECATS | TROPHIC MATTERS (FOOD AND FORAGING)

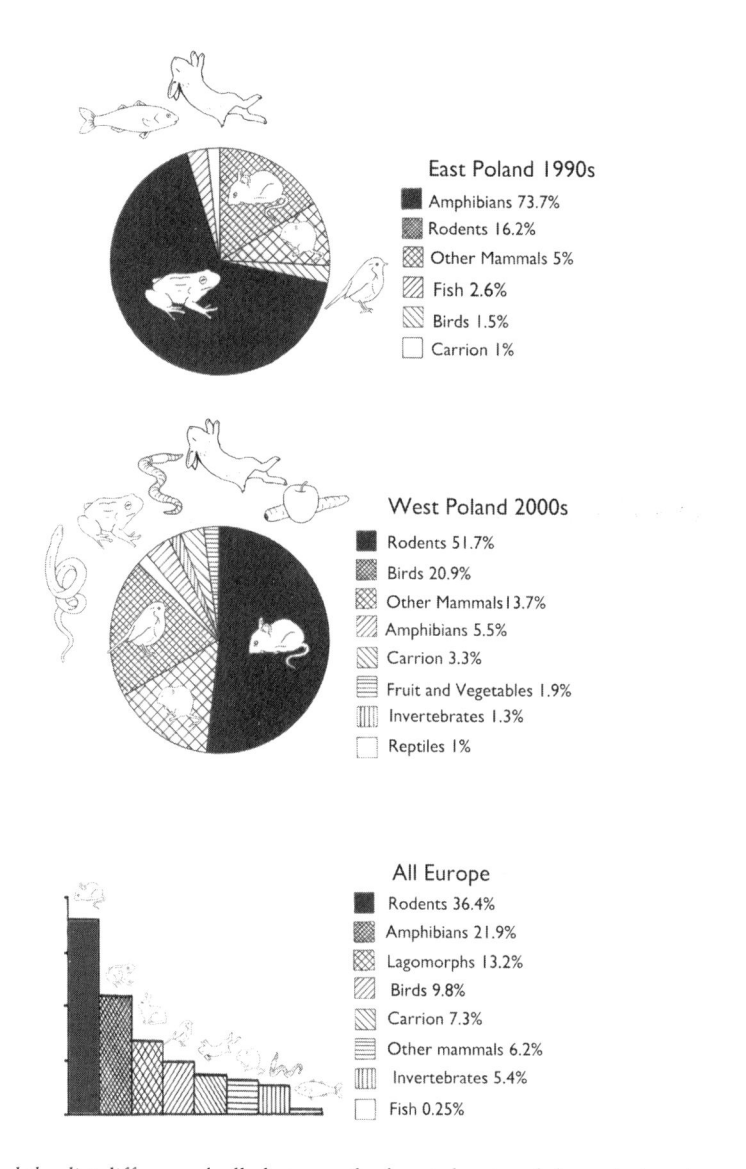

East Poland 1990s
- Amphibians 73.7%
- Rodents 16.2%
- Other Mammals 5%
- Fish 2.6%
- Birds 1.5%
- Carrion 1%

West Poland 2000s
- Rodents 51.7%
- Birds 20.9%
- Other Mammals 13.7%
- Amphibians 5.5%
- Carrion 3.3%
- Fruit and Vegetables 1.9%
- Invertebrates 1.3%
- Reptiles 1%

All Europe
- Rodents 36.4%
- Amphibians 21.9%
- Lagomorphs 13.2%
- Birds 9.8%
- Carrion 7.3%
- Other mammals 6.2%
- Invertebrates 5.4%
- Fish 0.25%

In Poland the diet differs markedly between the forested east and the agricultural west. The dominance of rodents and amphibians in polecat diets across Europe shows how atypical British polecats are with their heavy emphasis on lagomorphs.

Forest where frogs and toads made up 74 per cent of polecat food, in those days polecats inhabiting Eurasia's extensive natural forests probably fed mainly upon such anuran amphibians, with woodland rodents such as the bank vole and wood mouse of secondary importance. Importantly, predation upon anurans is not restricted to the prey's spring and summer activity period because polecats can reportedly extract hibernating amphibians from their muddy hibernacula. This explains why such prey may still dominate the polecat's diet in the winter months, such as in Mette Hammershoj's study in Jutland in Denmark, where amphibians were the dominant prey item in 87 per cent of polecat guts.

This pre-historic focus upon anurans, still commonly apparent today even in deforested landscapes, sets the polecat apart from many other European predators and, with certain skilful patterns of polecat behaviour linked specifically to anuran predation, suggests a hint of dietary specialism in what is otherwise a generalist predator. For example, unlike most other predators, polecats are able to catch, skin and consume common toads without ingesting their poisonous skins; and where there is a tempting surplus of adult anurans, such as at traditional spawning sites in the spring, reportedly they may cache many live frogs and toads by paralysing them with a bite at the base of the skull, so that they stay fresh in a den or underground food store (though it is not certain whether this paralysing bite is a deliberate 'fresh food' storage strategy or simply a beneficial chance effect).

Further evidence of the polecat's special toad-handling skills comes from a comparative study of the diets of eight mustelid species across several districts in Belarus in the 1990s by Vadim Sidorovich: he found that although all the semi-aquatic mustelids (polecat, American mink, European mink and otter) preyed on both frogs and toads to some extent, only the polecat consumed both species in proportion to their abundance in his study areas; in contrast the otter and both mink species took proportionately many more frogs than toads, which they consumed only rarely presumably because of their poisonous skins; so the polecat was the only one not avoiding consumption of toads, meaning that it enjoys an advantage over its mustelid competitors in Belarus and, probably, in many other parts of its range.

A herpetologist friend, Nigel Hand, made a gruesome discovery at a

Herefordshire amphibian spawning pond one spring that was probably the work of a polecat: over a hundred adult common toads had been neatly skinned from the ankles upwards and all the flesh on the hind legs and around the hips had been consumed, leaving much of the rest of the animals intact at the pond's margins (a few were even still alive); whichever animal was responsible for such skilful but wasteful butchery (polecat is the most likely candidate), it had carefully avoided encountering the poison-producing parotoid glands behind each toad's head. Otters sometimes feast on toads at British spawning sites but, according to my late friend Rob Strachan, they tend to skin the whole animal and eat more than just the flesh off the legs, leaving the bizarre sight of several inside-out toad skins around the edge of a pond with few other remains.

So the polecat may once have been more of an anuran specialist in the days before we humans cleared the wildwood and drained the land to grow crops and graze our livestock. Clever toad-handling skills and winter access to hibernacula secured a competitive advantage that may still benefit polecats today in certain circumstances. This cunning specialism nestles like a secret weapon within the polecat's generalist predatory armoury, a feature that it shares with another 'specialist/generalist' mustelid across the Atlantic: the fisher *Martes pennanti* is a generalist North American, marten-like predator that has developed the unique ability to kill porcupines so that, when other prey become scarce, it gains special access to prickly meals that other predators have to avoid. However, despite its useful anti-toad specialism, it is the polecat's innate predatory flexibility that has enabled it to cope with the many anthropogenic changes in habitats and prey availability over the millennia, so that today we regard it as a true generalist; and now, on the north-western edge of its range, such opportunism has enabled the polecat to take advantage of the British rabbit bonanza.

An easier life in Britain thanks to rabbits? We humans have, inadvertently, made life rather easier for the polecat in Britain by providing some abundant sources of wild prey that would not otherwise have been present: we deliberately introduced the rabbit in the twelfth century and accidentally allowed the brown rat to colonise these islands from the 1720s. Both these mammals achieve high population densities in modern

British landscapes – diseases and human control permitting – and both are major agricultural pests. Nevertheless, they represent a valuable ecological resource for polecats (and several other predators); and the ever-present rabbit, in particular, sets Britain apart from Continental Eurasia where that species is either much scarcer or, in the east, completely absent. Rabbits provide an abundant source of prey that polecats seem perfectly designed to exploit, and their burrows offer safe daytime resting sites for polecats in intensively managed agricultural landscapes where suitable shelter (and other prey) is sometimes scarce. Consequently, British polecats seem able to thrive wherever wild rabbits are reasonably common, and this brings advantages not enjoyed by polecats elsewhere in Europe.

Importantly, the 'rabbit option' has freed polecats in Britain from the partial dependence upon wetland habitats and prey that characterises their Continental ecology; in turn this reduces competition between polecats and American mink in Britain, something that has reportedly contributed to the decline of polecats in some countries such as Poland and Belarus (where rabbits are absent); it also means that in Britain our polecats are less constrained, in terms of the habitats they can occupy, so long as rabbits remain a common and widespread source of food. That is something we

Where wild rabbits are common, polecats spend a lot of their time hunting them underground in their burrows, which also provide safe den sites for tired polecats.

cannot take for granted because of the understandable interest in reducing the impact of wild rabbits upon agricultural productivity: memories of the first devastating outbreak of *Myxomatosis* in the early 1950s remind us how a vast biomass of rabbit prey could be swiftly removed by disease over a very wide area, especially if helped by deliberate human spread.

So, while polecat populations are struggling in many parts of Continental Europe for a variety of reasons linked to modern agriculture and invasive species, polecats in Britain are thriving in comparison, partly thanks to our dense and widespread populations of wild rabbits. It is interesting to speculate how polecats in Britain would have fared without rabbits, especially during the dark days of post-1950s biodiversity loss, when agricultural intensification and land drainage did so much harm to wildlife habitats: inevitably polecats would have remained more dependent upon dwindling wetlands and declining prey such as amphibians and water voles; they would have faced much fiercer competition for scarce resources with the invasive American mink, which was able to colonise our waterways so easily because we had largely eradicated its two most effective native competitors (the polecat and the otter).

Such effects may already operate in some parts of Britain because rabbits are not abundant in all habitats: they tend to avoid our rain-soaked boggy uplands and areas with heavy clay-based soils in the lowlands, so polecats here may struggle for the reasons given above; we should expect them to thrive best on the lighter, free-draining, diggable soils most favoured by rabbits. Despite these habitat variations I cannot imagine that our polecats could have achieved their strong population recovery in the late twentieth century and beyond without the humble rabbit lending a helping paw. And if for any reason rabbits in Britain become scarce once more, we have to expect our polecats to suffer the worrying declines reported on the Continent.

POLECAT HABITATS

Broad habitat selection
Considering the wide range of prey species consumed by polecats it comes as no surprise that they are able to live in many different habitats and landscape types across their European range: they occur in all types of woodland and farmland, hedgerows and scrub, moorland, mountains, marshland and bogs, river valleys, coastal fringes, cliffs, sand dunes, farmsteads, villages and suburban areas; in fact, the only terrestrial habitat in which the polecat seems unable to establish and maintain populations is the centre of towns and cities, where prey densities are too low and traffic densities (and associated polecat mortality) are too high for the species to survive. Within this broad suite, of course, there are some habitats that are favoured over others, usually because they support a greater biomass or diversity of polecat prey, and this is reflected in the varying population densities at which polecats live in different habitats: prey-rich habitats support more polecats because each individual needs a smaller home range to support itself than it would in relatively prey-poor habitats.

Within Continental Europe many studies have shown that the polecat is closely associated with riparian habitats such as the margins of rivers, streams, lakes and ponds. For example, Carlo Rondinini radio-tracked polecats in a fragmented agricultural landscape in the Abruzzo Region of the Apennine Mountains in Central Italy: here he found a strong habitat preference for ponds and riparian vegetation that he explained in terms of foraging for favoured prey (anurans and small rodents) and the polecat's innate need to stick to cover in otherwise more open landscapes (with riparian vegetation providing valuable connectivity across the landscape).

In striking contrast to the European pattern, here in Britain the polecat shows no preference for damp and watery places. There could be several reasons for this difference: firstly, it could be due to the 'rabbit factor'; wild rabbits are more abundant and widespread in Britain than in the rest of the polecat's range – indeed they are absent from most of the eastern half of the polecat's entire Palearctic distribution – so polecats on the Continent are much more dependent upon other sources of prey such as amphibians and rodents associated with river valleys, other wetlands and damp woodlands; secondly, the polecat's non-association with wetlands here may also be a consequence of the poor quality of wetland habitats in the intensively farmed landscapes of modern Britain, where the riparian fringe along our over-engineered rivers and streams is very narrow and supports limited prey resources when compared with the more natural, extensive wetlands found in Continental Europe; and finally, polecats in Britain may be forced to avoid wetland habitats in order to reduce competition with the widespread and ecologically very similar American mink.

Habitat preferences on lowland farmland

The VWT's radio-tracking study of polecats on lowland farmland in the west of England revealed some clear patterns of habitat use: across the whole year polecats spent 36 per cent of their time in field boundaries (mainly hedgerows), 35 per cent of their time in woodland or scrub, 23 per cent in farmyards and farm buildings, and 6 per cent in other, minor habitats (such as suburban or wetland areas). However, this pattern of use showed seasonal variation: in the 'summer' half of the year (April to September) polecats spent 52 per cent of their time in field boundaries and 44 per cent of their time in woodland/scrub, with only 1 per cent spent in farmyards and farm buildings and 3 per cent in other habitats; in the 'winter' half of the year (October to March) time in farmyards and farm buildings leapt up to 31 per cent (linked with winter predation on farmyard rats), on a par with time spent in woodland/scrub and field boundaries, while 7 per cent of time was spent in other, minor habitats.

The figures for percentage use of habitats such as those above tell us where polecats spend their time in the farmed landscape, but they don't reveal much about habitat preferences; these can be teased out by a technique called Compositional Analysis, which my friend Liz Halliwell kindly helped me with. Compositional Analysis takes account of the differing extent of all habitats within a study area, so that an animal's time spent in each is linked to its availability, which in turn reveals how much it is preferred or avoided; it also provides a ranking of all habitats from the most preferred to the most avoided. The radio-tagged polecats in my VWT study area in the west of England showed some very clear preferences for the seven main habitats present. In order of preference year-round, and starting with the most preferred habitat, these were: (1) Woodland Edge (the peripheral 5 metres of woodland, plantation or scrub); (2) Agricultural Premises (farmyards and farm buildings); (3) Field Boundaries (usually hedgerows); (4) Wetlands (rivers, streams, lakes, ponds, marshes etc.); (5) Woodland (all but the peripheral 5 metres); (6) Suburban (villages); and (7) Open Fields.

So my polecats showed the clearest preferences for the edges of woodland and scrub and for farmyards and farm buildings; field boundaries such as hedgerows came third. I was pretty sure these preferences reflected the polecats' foraging and dietary priorities directed towards rabbits and rodents because, in my study area, rabbit burrows were concentrated along woodland edges and hedgerows, and rats were concentrated in the farmyards. Interestingly, when a winter-only sample of the radio-tracking data was examined, the ranking of the top two preferred habitats was reversed, doubtless reflecting the polecats' more intensive foraging for farmyard rodents in the winter months.

Microhabitat selection

Beyond the broad patterns of habitat use by polecats apparent at a landscape scale, habitat selection may be influenced at a much finer level than is possible to detect via radio-tracking studies, as revealed by Darius Weber in his exploration of microhabitat use by polecats in Switzerland. Noting that several radio-tracking studies had reported a preference among polecats for densely structured habitats such as woodland and scrub, and an avoidance of open habitats such as the middle of agricultural fields, Weber set out to discover experimentally, by observing hand-reared young polecats in an enclosure where he could manipulate the nature, extent and distribution of cover, what patterns of microhabitat selection might be operating within those densely structured habitats. In Weber's generally well-wooded enclosure the young polecats showed a powerful innate preference for microhabitats that concealed them from view, such as dense vegetation or other material at ground level. This confirmed the endearingly simple observations of Goethe, writing in 1940, that his hand-reared polecats were visibly excited by 'being in something' or 'being under something' (behaviour with which ferret-keepers will be familiar).

Darius Weber suggests there are two important survival benefits that explain the polecat's innate selection for dense ground cover: foraging success and predation avoidance. In his radio-tracking studies in Switzerland Weber found that, away from farm buildings, frogs and toads were the most important polecat prey, with mice, voles and shrews of minor importance; although the association of anurans with dense ground cover is not clear, small mammals clearly do prefer such habitats, so Weber concluded that foraging for generally small prey may partly explain the polecat's microhabitat preference. He makes a more convincing case for predation avoidance being the driving force behind polecats selecting habitats that offer thorough concealment opportunities, reminding us that, despite their impressive 'stink defence', polecats are killed by a wide range of predators, including large birds of prey such as golden eagles and eagle owls that would be relatively less affected by defensive odours than would the mammalian predators.

Suburban and 'garden decking' polecats

Although the polecats in my rural VWT radio-tracking study showed an avoidance of suburban habitat comprising the two villages in the study area, there are many recent examples of polecats living successfully within the edges of towns and cities in England and Wales. While it is tempting to dismiss such reports as most probably involving escaped ferrets, visual evidence in the form of photographs and video clips confirms that they are frequently true polecats. During the VWT's distribution survey of 2004–2006 (from which most of the information in this section is derived) there were 68 records of possible polecats seen in gardens, many of which were in suburbia; and around the same time Sue Tatman of Cheshire Wildlife Trust gathered many further reports of garden polecats, especially from the southern suburbs of Manchester. So why are these polecats living in suburbia? What sources of food are they finding and what sort of dens are they resting in?

Of the sightings of polecats in gardens 63 per cent occurred in the late summer months of July to September (this must be influenced by the fact that people spend more time in their gardens at this time of year, as well as by the greater daytime activity of breeding female polecats in summer, which makes them and their kits more visible), and many related to successful breeding in or beneath garages, sheds, conservatories and other outhouses; some mother polecats took advantage of the early 2000s householder habit of building trendy wooden decking in gardens by giving birth to their litters in the sheltered spaces beneath. (I was shown delightful photographs of

POLECATS | POLECAT HABITATS

Polecats sometimes breed in suburban gardens, where gaps under decking and garden sheds provide safe den sites.

decking polecat litters from both Kidderminster and Droitwich.) So even in our small, modern suburban gardens there are plenty of suitable den sites in which polecats can rest and breed.

Polecats would not choose to occupy suburban areas if there was not sufficient suitable food available for them. Many householders reported that 'their' polecats were seen to eat food put out at night for cats, foxes and hedgehogs (the advent of affordable motion-sensitive camera traps means that such behaviour can be recorded faithfully while we sleep soundly in our beds); some people put out food for the polecats once they realised they were there; there were some reports of successful predation of wild prey in gardens, including rabbits, frogs and a blackbird; two reports related to attempted predation of pets and poultry in gardens; and in five cases polecats (or were they ferrets?) took shameful advantage of human hospitality by entering houses through a cat flap or other opening!

Despite the many reports of them scavenging food put out in gardens, it is highly likely that our suburban polecats are also exploiting more natural sources of prey: populations of rabbits, small mammals, amphibians and birds thrive in low density residential urban areas, especially where modern approaches to town planning now retain rough green spaces between the more traditional habitat corridors along rivers, canals and railway lines.

Although polecats have lived close to human dwellings for centuries in rural areas, reports of suburban polecats are a relatively new phenomenon. This is partly because the species has only recently spread from the sparsely human-populated hills of Wales and the West of England into the busier lowlands where more of us live, and where our towns and cities sprawl and merge conveniently with polecat-friendly farmland. But there are surely other recent changes that could also explain this trend: our passion for feeding garden birds year-round, and our rediscovered interest in home-composting and poultry-keeping all serve to boost populations of rodents in and around our gardens, with knock-on benefits to rodent predators like the polecat; our interest in wildlife gardening must promote species that could end up as tasty polecat snacks; and thanks to our general support for wildlife conservation we are much more tolerant (cat-flap invasions excepted) and aware of interesting species sharing our living space than were our ancestors, who would probably have called swiftly for a trap or shotgun to deal with any garden polecat spotted in or before the mid 1900s.

WORK, REST AND PLAY

Dens

Outside the mating season an adult polecat divides its time between foraging, resting and defending its patch against other polecats. Familiarity with the location of resources, such as safe den sites and good foraging areas, is crucial to survival and is the main reason why each polecat occupies a stable home range or territory. Like most

Polecats are slim enough to occupy dens in all sorts of places such as gaps in stone walls.

carnivores, polecats spend as much as three-quarters of their time sleeping and resting, so secure, sheltered dens are very important to them. However, there is nothing very distinctive about their dens, so the only certain way to identify them is to observe a polecat entering or leaving one; consequently most of what we know about polecat dens comes from radio-tracking studies in which animals are followed and located accurately while they are sleeping.

Polecats rarely dig their own dens because they usually don't need to and they are not great diggers anyway. In his study of polecats in Switzerland, Darius Weber did record a few dens that were probably dug by polecats, such as among tree roots or in piles of soft earth; these dens were simple burrows rarely more than half a metre long, and in some cases the polecat had merely enlarged a space that was already there.

Fortunately for polecats in Britain the countryside and much of suburbia is liberally supplied with dry, draught-free, polecat-sized cavities at or below ground level (another advantage of being relatively small and sinuous) ranging from rabbit burrows, through holes among tree roots, rocks and stone walls, to gaps beneath garden sheds or in stacks of hay and straw. Unfussy as ever, polecats may use a huge variety of such places in which to sleep and breed, with rabbit burrows by far the most popular in the radio-tracking studies carried out by Philip Blandford in mid Wales (49 per cent of 106 polecat dens identified) and by the VWT in western England (80 per cent). Every one of my radio-tagged polecats in the 1990s VWT study made use of rabbit burrows as daytime resting sites.

One reason for this preference for rabbit burrows must be the combination of shelter and food that they offer, because wherever wild rabbits are present they are the polecat's favoured prey. Since most polecat predation of rabbits happens underground in their burrows, it makes sense for the successful hunter to stay put to consume the carcass in shelter and safety; what could be more convenient than that – Bed, Breakfast and Evening Meal?! I could usually tell when a radio-tagged polecat had made a kill underground, because it would usually remain in the same rabbit burrow for up to three days.

Den type	% occurrence
Rabbit burrow	80.1
Farmyard barn/shed/haystack	10.2
Farmyard scrap	4.3
Drainage pipe	2.1
Tree roots	1.6
Isolated barn/shed/haystack	1.1
Domestic garage	0.5

The proportion of identifiable den types used by radio-tagged polecats during a VWT study in Herefordshire and Worcestershire in the 1990s (n=186).

Sometimes polecats may use less sheltered, above-ground resting sites in vegetation away from buildings, although I have never witnessed this myself. In his study in Switzerland Darius Weber found polecats sleeping in various types of vegetation, including in thickets, piles of grass and branches, stacks of firewood, and in a hollow tree, but always in situations where the polecat was well hidden. He noted that in some situations they constructed spherical nests of dry grass and moss beneath piles of other vegetation.

Each polecat may use several different dens scattered over its home range; their locations and patterns of use are mainly linked to foraging activity, enabling polecats to avoid travelling too far between bouts of hunting and resting. In the VWT study in the west of England 13 polecats each used between 4 and 22 dens over radio-tracking periods of 19–47 days; at the extreme end three males each used more than 20 dens, one of which used 22 different dens in 27 days. This young male was radio-tracked in September and October so had most likely only just settled into his new home range having dispersed from his natal range. His almost daily shifts to a new den probably reflected his need to get to know his new home patch as quickly as possible, as well as defending it against other polecats looking for a place to settle. In mid winter polecats tended to shift between dens rather less frequently.

The only other obvious seasonal shift in patterns of den use that I spotted was in the winter months, when radio-tagged polecats were more likely to be found sleeping in barns, sheds and haystacks in farmyards, usually in association with predation upon concentrations of rats and mice. In my experience there was no link between cold spells and a polecat's tendency to sleep in farm buildings. Darius Weber noted a similar pattern in Switzerland, but he interpreted the winter use of buildings as being driven by the polecat's need for shelter in cold weather rather than its predation of commensal rodents. Weber also found that polecat occupation of less sheltered above ground den sites in vegetation was typical of the warmer summer months and was rare in winter.

Activity patterns

Polecats are pretty strictly nocturnal for most of the year, with most foraging and travelling activity occurring under cover of darkness; only in mid summer, when the extra pressures of childcare force mother polecats to forage both by night and day, is daytime activity commonly observed. This predominantly nocturnal tendency is probably driven by two factors: the need for polecats to coincide their activity with that of their prey, and predation avoidance. The historical significance in the polecat's diet of anuran amphibians, which are only active at night, together with woodland rodents that are similarly inclined, has probably influenced the timing of polecat activity for thousands of years. Also the need to avoid attacks by large diurnal birds of prey and, more recently, by humans and their dogs, is a good reason to lie low during daylight. A strictly nocturnal lifestyle is especially important where polecats choose to live and forage close to dwellings occupied by intolerant humans, as they have done for centuries.

There are some situations where polecats (other than breeding females) may choose to forage during daylight: this is when prey may be captured in thick cover or even underground. In my VWT radio-tracking study 28 per cent of recorded polecat activity occurred during daytime and it almost always involved animals out of sight: in farmyards daytime activity comprised just 11 per cent of total activity and only ever involved polecats within barns or haystacks; away from farmyards daytime activity mainly involved polecats underground in rabbit burrows or above ground within woodland and scrub.

RELATIONS WITH OTHER CARNIVORES

One challenge facing the polecat as it spreads back into its former range is to compete successfully with other carnivores so as to gain access to all the resources it needs to sustain itself year-round, such as den sites, foraging areas and prey. We call the suite of potentially competing carnivore species that coexist in an area a 'guild', and the success of each species in the guild depends upon how effectively it can secure a share of the resources it needs through competition or competition-avoidance. The polecat in Britain shares a terrestrial/aquatic guild with the otter and American mink, with the stoat perhaps playing a minor role at the terrestrial end. Because our polecat and the American mink are so similar in size, shape and generalist predatory behaviour one would predict especially fierce competition between them.

The similarity of mink and polecat dentition (teeth are a crucial determinant of prey size selection in mustelids) led researchers Dayan and Simberloff to speculate that the invasive mink probably grabbed part or all of the ecological niche previously vacated by the persecuted polecat in Britain; in which case the mink's swift invasion of our waterways in the 1960s and 70s was partly facilitated by we humans having helpfully eradicated the polecat a few decades earlier; then we made life even easier for the mink by accidentally poisoning our otters with agricultural chemicals from the 1950s onwards, so that the much larger and competitively dominant otter was conveniently in rapid retreat while mink were spreading along our rivers and streams. So, having unkindly confined our American guests in small cages before turning them into fur coats, we soon made amends by making it extraordinarily easy for their descendants to establish expanding, breeding populations in the wild. Now that they are 'over here and over-sexed' (as we said of GIs during World War II); and, predicting that competition with the polecat is likely, it follows that the widespread presence of American mink in Britain could make life very tough for the returning polecat.

Some evidence of an adverse impact of invasive American mink upon polecats comes from studies in Belarus by Vadim Sidorovich: he noted that after American mink arrived in his study area the numbers of both European polecats and European mink were reduced and the sex ratios of their populations changed, with females being the main losers in both species; in polecats the adult sex ratio shifted from 59 per cent to 95 per cent males in response to the establishment of mink. Sidorovich also found that, while male polecats remained the same size after the arrival of mink, average female polecat body size increased, perhaps because smaller females were more likely to die in the presence of invasive mink. A widescale study by Rafael Barrientos suggests that the sex ratio distortion caused by invasive American mink now occurs in polecat populations across Europe: he scrutinised 71 datasets from 21 countries (including Britain) comprising more than 10,000 polecats and found that, in areas where feral mink are established, the polecat adult sex ratio was more skewed towards males than in areas where mink are absent. In conservation terms this reduction in the number of adult females may have serious consequences for polecat population dynamics and reproductive output with, among other things, the likelihood of increased competition among males for access to scarce females during the mating season.

Studying the processes involved in competition between elusive carnivores in the wild is notoriously difficult, but researchers at Oxford University's WildCRU (Wildlife Conservation Research Unit) have risen to the challenge in respect of the American mink and polecat in Britain. Lauren Harrington found that, although mink and polecats occupied the same parts of her upper Thames valley study area and had overlapping home ranges, they appeared to reduce competition for food and avoid encounters by being active at different times: polecats were mainly nocturnal and mink were only active by day. Interestingly this diurnal behaviour, which had previously been unusual in mink in Britain, was not reported by Nobby Yamaguchi in his earlier study of the same mink population in the 1990s before polecats arrived in the area, so it might have been a competition-avoidance response either to the arrival of

polecats or to the arrival of otters that (irritatingly, in scientific terms) returned to that part of the Thames Valley at about the same time as the polecats.

The widespread presence of American mink in Britain has not yet, apparently, prevented or hindered the steady recovery of the polecat, suggesting that the two species are able to coexist by means of competition avoidance; this situation seems to contrast with that in Belarus where adverse impacts upon polecats were clearly significant. Lauren Harrington explains this apparent contradiction by pointing out that, firstly, American mink in Vadim Sidorovich's near-pristine marshland study area in Belarus occupy wider home ranges than the narrow riparian fringe to which they are restricted in intensively farmed Britain, so the scope for competition avoidance by polecats is seriously reduced; secondly, polecats in Britain are significantly larger than those in Belarus, so are less likely to be at risk during direct encounters with American mink; finally, there are no wild rabbits in Belarus, so polecats there are less able to avoid competing with mink for wetland prey than they are in Britain.

Encouragingly, there are places where polecats and American mink may coexist despite the complete absence of rabbits. In Jutland, a rabbit-free part of Denmark, Mette Hammershoj studied the winter diets of both polecats and mink and found some striking differences: while polecats preyed mainly on amphibians with some mammals but very few birds and fish, the mink spread their attention more evenly across mammals, birds, fish and amphibians. This difference in dietary focus may be sufficient to reduce competition between these two mustelids to an acceptable level but, for the polecat at least, it depends upon the widespread availability of healthy amphibian populations – not something we can take for granted in many modern agricultural landscapes.

Despite the encouraging evidence of coexistence of polecats and American mink (which have now been unnaturally thrown together in the wild in many European countries because of our past desire for fur coats and the mink's equally keen desire to escape from captivity), the two species are so similar in ecological terms that some competition between them is extremely likely. We need to keep a close eye on this issue in Britain because future changes in climate, habitats and prey availability, or subtle shifts in the composition of the carnivore guild and the behaviour of its members, could reduce the scope for competition avoidance and lead to adverse impacts upon polecat populations.

SELF-DEFENCE

A pungently effective defence weapon is one key to the polecat's survival and success (though it doesn't work against its main modern predators – motor vehicles, poisons and traps). Evolving in the European wildwood populated by wolves, brown bears, lynx and assorted other dangerous carnivores, all small animals needed strategies to reduce the risk of becoming a tasty snack for the bigger ones; even small carnivores like the polecat have to avoid being killed as food or as a competitor by larger members of the European carnivore guild. So, while the hedgehog was developing its spiny cloak, and the pine marten was learning how to climb out of danger, the polecat's cunning plan was to invest in a spectacularly stinky bottom.

The polecat's defence system is two-pronged, with front and rear components: at the front it has sharp teeth and a powerful bite that helps to deter those aggressors that fail to heed its startling 'chack' warning sound (like a short, high-pitched bark); and rearwards it has two glands the size of large peas just inside its anus that are capable of emitting a volatile, pungent stench of awesome deterrent potential. The odour is reminiscent of concentrated burnt rubber with intense musky overtones and a lingering 'scorched throat' aftertaste (as a wine taster might say). Of course this defence works best if the scent can be spread widely and, if possible, directed towards the opponent's nose, so when threatened by an attacker (or if stressed in other ways or injured) a polecat manoeuvres itself to present its rear end towards the source of danger; sometimes it performs a 'tail waggle' involving a sideways shake of the tail from the base so as to spread the emerging scent; and if circumstances permit it may even perform a skunk-like handstand to get its rear weapon as close as possible to a taller attacker.

Almost all of my close encounters with wild polecats have involved animals that I caught in cage traps as part of my study with the VWT. This is a scary situation for any wild animal, especially when a human approaches the trap and the captive is unable to retreat to safety; in such situations a polecat may become very stressed, will emit the loud 'chack' warning and release its stink defence. The best way to limit the animal's stress is to provide material for it to hide among inside the trap (I always covered the traps with dry hay, which a trapped polecat could pull inside the trap to make a nest to hide in) and to keep the trap covered as much as possible; it also helps to keep calm and quiet when close to an occupied trap. I quickly learnt to read the behavioural warning signs and thereby avoided frequent exposure to the defensive stink and permanent damage to my sense of smell; once the tail waggling started I knew I had got it wrong!

Beyond the artificial situation of an animal restrained in a live-trap, naturalists and researchers rarely have the opportunity to witness a polecat defending itself, but an incident described to me in the 1990s by John Davies, then warden of Cors Carron National Nature Reserve in Wales, shows just how effective the anti-predator defence can be: John was walking his two dogs over the reserve one Sunday morning when they encountered a male polecat among some sparse lowland heath vegetation; outnumbered and with nowhere suitable to hide the polecat was quickly cornered by the dogs, a collie and a Labrador, which worked as a team in attacking and trying to kill the animal; each time one gripped the polecat in its jaws it quickly dropped it because of the powerful stink, which soon pervaded the whole area; this pattern continued for several minutes, with the polecat's sharp teeth and stink defence repeatedly repelling the two dogs; eventually the dogs gave up and left the animal alive and relatively unharmed; and afterwards, according to John, the distinctive odour of polecat could be smelt on the dogs' fur for many days! This observation shows us why polecats have rather little to fear from wild predators such as foxes, which may have an impact upon the populations of other small mustelids having less effective defence systems, such as stoats and pine martens.

SICK BAY OR HEALTH MATTERS

Parasites
In common with other mammals, polecats play host to a range of ectoparasites such as fleas and ticks, as well as worm-like helminth endoparasites including cestodes, nematodes and trematodes; most of these have little or no impact upon the health of polecats that are otherwise in good condition. One helminth worm commonly found in the intestines of wild polecats, mink and, occasionally, domestic cats, is *Aonchotheca putorii*, which seems to claim a special connection with the polecat through its specific name.

The most visible affliction on live or freshly killed polecats is the burden of adult ticks that some animals carry around the ears and between their shoulder blades (exactly where it is hardest to scratch with their hind feet); the one found most commonly on the polecat is the hedgehog tick, *Ixodes hexagonus*, which, despite its name, is found on many different mammals; as well as carrying many ticks at different stages of their life cycle, polecats often bear unsightly clusters of ten or more pale grey adult ticks. Soon after a polecat dies the ectoparasites tend to depart in search of a new, live host, so few are found on road casualties that have been dead for more than a day or two. Adult ticks are most visible on polecats when they are in summer pelage, because the fur is relatively short and sparse so the parasites show up more clearly.

One of the more beastly nematode parasites that the polecat has to cope with is the almost unpronounceable *Skrjabingylus nasicola*, which, as its name suggests, infects the animal's nose (it is also found in stoats and weasels). This tiny worm lives in the polecat's nasal and ethmoid sinuses (cavities inside the bones of the nose and around the eyes), where it causes erosion or abnormal growth of the bones that may lead to death in extreme cases.

Diseases and other ailments
In common with the domestic ferret, polecats may suffer from distemper, influenza and pneumonia, although compared with captive ferrets it has not been so easy to study their prevalence and effects in wild polecats. Polecats may also carry diseases such as toxoplasmosis, leptospirosis,

trichinosis and adiaspiromycosis (a fungal infection of the lungs).

Rabies has been reported from polecats in parts of Central and Eastern Europe and Russia, usually at low levels, although a study in the Bryansk region of Russia suggests that where polecat populations overlap with those of raccoon dogs and foxes in rugged landscapes polecats may account for more than half of all wildlife cases of rabies. With such high prevalence among polecats in an area – and this doesn't seem to be typical of other parts of Europe where rabies is established in wildlife – there is scope for the polecat population to act as a passive store of rabies infection between outbreaks.

Bovine tuberculosis (bTB) is a serious problem for cattle farmers in Britain, where debate has raged about how best to tackle the disease in the 'wildlife reservoir' and among badgers in particular. A recent study by Richard Delahay and colleagues confirmed bTB in a wide range of British mammals in the south-west of England, including in a polecat (just one out of 24 polecats sampled proved positive). A simple risk assessment carried out as part of that study, based on bTB prevalence levels, population densities and patterns of behaviour relating to cattle, suggests that the polecat's risk score (indicating its likely significance in the transmission of bTB to cattle) is relatively low compared with deer and badgers. Bovine TB has also been reported in feral ferrets in New Zealand, where its prevalence in ferrets may reach 66 per cent in areas where cattle are infected (although possums are usually the main wildlife vector). Just like polecats in Britain, feral ferrets in New Zealand spend some of their time in farmyards where cattle are housed and their food is stored; one can envisage routes via which bTB could be transmitted between cattle and the ferrets and vice versa, especially where the ferrets sleep in stacks of hay which is then fed to the cattle.

Tail alopecia or The mystery of male baldness!

One of the great unsolved polecat mysteries concerns the cause of alopecia or hair loss on the tails of some animals. This condition typically leaves the tail in a partly bald state along most of its length, usually with a sparse scatter of bristly guard hairs and a rough, scaly appearance to the skin, often with many 'blackheads' (blocked pores) visible. The condition occurs in ferrets too, and affected animals are referred to as 'rat-tailed ferrets' for obvious reasons. Although it looks unpleasant the condition is harmless, unlike some causes of hair loss in other mammals, such as sarcoptic mange. Ferret-keepers have tried all sorts of nutritional, medical and dermatological remedies with no clear benefit.

Ferret-keepers report the condition occurring in both sexes, although predominantly in males; in wild polecats I have only ever seen it in adult males in summer pelage, when it affects up to 10 per cent of the male population. Tail alopecia is apparently temporary and seasonal because affected animals grow normal fur on their tails once more when they next moult into their winter coats in the autumn; but they are likely to lose their fur again the following summer.

CAUSES OF INJURY AND DEATH

The polecat's defensive stink, which has protected it against predators for millennia, is pretty useless today against the modern man-made threats of cars, rodenticides and spring traps. These charming human inventions are probably the main causes of injury and death for polecats in Britain today, although comparing the numerical contributions of each is difficult because road casualties are much more likely to be detected than are polecats dying from a poison overdose or killed in traps on private land. However, we can congratulate ourselves upon the huge reduction in the deliberate killing of polecats compared with the early 1900s, although in parts of mid Wales some farmers still kill polecats in the belief that they are a threat to lambs.

Polecats and roads – a love-hate relationship?
Roads are both good and bad for polecats: the road surface provides a nightly smörgåsbord of easily gathered live food in the form of slow-moving amphibians on wet nights in spring and autumn, and abundant fresh carrion such as roadkill rabbits and pheasants; by searching along roads at night, a nocturnal carnivore like the polecat is well-placed to dine on these 'Tarmac Tapas' at their freshest; also, roadside habitats such as rough grassland, scrub and hedgerows may represent the best foraging corridors for polecats in intensively farmed, 'over-tidy' landscapes, offering more tempting concentrations of prey compared with the surrounding farmland; but on the down side, busy roads offer the frequent threat of death or injury beneath the wheels of vehicles speeding home at night – unlike its diurnal corvid competitors, the polecat cannot easily evade the fast cars heading home from the pub.

The pursuit of easy prey is one reason why so many polecats are killed by vehicles on our roads. (Could it be the 'driving' factor in polecat mortality?!) This was confirmed by a study in central Spain by Barrientos and Bolonio, who showed that polecat road casualties were more likely to occur on stretches of road with abundant rabbit burrows nearby (as in Britain, rabbits are important prey for polecats in Spain). They suggested three reasons why rabbits may choose to excavate warrens in roadside habitats: firstly, cuttings and embankments offer convenient, well-drained

POLECATS | CAUSES OF INJURY AND DEATH

places for digging burrows, often with good vegetation cover; secondly, compared with farmland nearby, roadsides carry less risk of damage to burrows by ploughing, cattle-trampling or other agricultural activities;

In midsummer, polecat families comprising mothers and up to ten juveniles may be seen crossing country roads in daytime.

finally, discharging firearms close to roads is illegal in Spain (and Britain) and the activity of many wild predators is reduced close to roads because of road traffic mortality or avoidance of disturbance, so roadsides tend to be safer places for breeding rabbit populations.

There is much evidence that polecats in Britain are drawn to roadside habitats just as they are in Spain. A study by Fred Slater of mammals using roads in mid Wales revealed that polecats were the fourth-commonest roadside scavenger after cats, foxes and badgers. Observations described in two of the VWT's surveys of polecats in Britain (1990–1997 and 2004–2006) show that the animals don't simply visit roads to find food; the surveys were based upon a wide-scale public appeal for records and observations of polecats, and many people reported encounters with live polecats on roads, mostly seen in car headlights at night. There were 113 separate observations falling into the categories shown in the table below. Other than individuals crossing roads, 28 per cent of reports related to animals seen foraging or feeding on or beside roads; and several sightings involved social activity such as playing, fighting or mating; 11 sightings were of family groups of a mother polecat with dependent young on roads – many of these were in daylight in mid summer when some mother polecats apparently use roads as a convenient route for moving their kits from one den to another.

Activities of polecats observed on or beside roads in Britain 1990–2006 (VWT data)	No. records	%
Crossing road	50	44.2
Foraging along road or roadside, eating on road or carrying prey	32	28.3
Family group on road	11	9.7
Two polecats playing, fighting or mating	11	9.7
Injured or orphaned polecat rescued from road	9	7.9
Total	113	

Considering the range of activities that polecats choose to indulge in on roads, it is no surprise that road casualties are a frequent cause of death for the species: the 1990s VWT survey revealed that road casualties comprised two thirds (67.6 per cent) of the 1,000+ polecat records received; and in the subsequent 2000s VWT survey the proportion of road casualties was even higher at 77 per cent of 1,200+ records. Jackie Underhill's study of mammals using roads in the English West Midlands gives a valuable insight into the likely impact of this toll upon the polecat population: she drove a 60-mile (96-kilometre) circuit on 52 days between February and November 1999 and recorded all the mammal road casualties; although polecats were recorded only three times as road casualties during this period, extrapolation of this figure to the national road network gives an estimate of 8,165 polecats killed per year on England's roads (this assumes that polecats are widespread in England, which is not yet the case, of course).

On this evidence it is reasonable to conclude that death on the roads is the dominant fate for polecats in Britain, but we should bear in mind that other forms of mortality are much less detectable and so are less likely to be recorded, such as deaths in traps and those caused by poisoning. Whatever their overall contribution to polecat mortality, in some circumstances roads and road traffic could have significant impacts upon polecat populations. For example, in areas where the density of roads and traffic is high, these may act as barriers to polecat dispersal because so few animals can pass through with their lives intact; worse still, where polecat mortality is consistently high due to road casualties, areas of high traffic density may represent 'population sinks' where a local polecat population either fails to establish or is permanently reduced because every year so many animals are ground into the asphalt. Possible evidence of this effect was reported by the VWT in the South Wales Valleys and around the West Midlands conurbation, where polecats in the 1990s apparently struggled to re-establish populations probably because of the high density of main roads. Also, patterns of spread by the recovering polecat population in the English Midlands suggest that large conurbations and associated transport networks, such as those between Liverpool and Manchester, have been constraining the northward expansion of the population.

On the subject of polecats safely crossing roads, a related concern is the recent tendency for highway engineers to install vertical concrete barriers (VCBs) along the middle of dual carriageways and motorways so as to reduce the risk of vehicle collisions between the two carriageways. With no gaps available, these represent a new and impassable barrier to small animals such as polecats, unlike the metal barrier fences that they replace, making it more likely that the animals would be killed by traffic as they search for a way around the barrier in the middle of the highway.

Secondary rodenticide poisoning

Another polecat foraging strategy with fatal consequences is the age-old pursuit of commensal rodents in and around farmyards. The polecat is one of a suite of predators that home in on infestations of rats and mice, especially in winter when rodent numbers peak in farm buildings full of stored grain, livestock food and hay. Farmers are obliged by law to control rodent pests, and the most popular method is deployment of anti-coagulant poisons in bait over an extended period. The rodents feed frequently on the poisoned bait and take several days to acquire a lethal dose; consequently such farmyards are populated by many rats and mice containing sub-lethal levels of poison before they eventually succumb. Modern rodenticides are persistent and highly toxic, so they pose a risk to predators foraging in rat-infested farmyards; the poison operates in the same way, interfering with the polecats' blood-clotting system so that they die from internal bleeding once a lethal dose has accumulated. It is an irresistible and deadly toxic trap.

A tendency for poisoned rodents to be easier to catch in the days before they die increases the likelihood that predators will acquire a lethal dose themselves. This 'Secondary Rodenticide Poisoning' has long been recognised as a cause of death in barn owls; but it was not until the 1990s that we began to understand the likely scale of its impact upon polecats. I was first alerted to the problem while radio-tracking polecats in Herefordshire as part of the VWT project: in autumn 1993 I was following a young female who foraged for rodents in two farmyards separated by about a kilometre; after a few weeks she was found dead by one of the farmers, without any external signs of injury, in her favourite farmyard where rodenticides were used to tackle the heavy rat infestation.

Suspecting accidental poisoning, I submitted her carcass to WIIS (the UK Government Wildlife Incident Investigation Scheme), which confirmed a liver residue of 1.4 milligrams per kilogram of difenacoum, the active ingredient of the rodenticide used on her favourite farm. Because of the lack of other information, this figure remains our best guide to the lethal level of this poison in wild polecats.

Something good came from the death of that young polecat, because it prompted a valuable collaboration between the VWT and vertebrate toxicologist Richard Shore of the Centre for Ecology and Hydrology, who led a series of studies to assess patterns of secondary rodenticide poisoning in polecats. Because polecats suffering from rodenticide poisoning tend to die out of sight in barns and haystacks on private land, it is difficult to confirm how many suffer this fate and what the lethal dose is; also, it means that this cause of death is greatly under-recorded compared with road casualties, for example. Our best evidence comes from rodenticide residues in the livers of road casualty polecats: Richard Shore's analysis in the 1990s showed that 46 per cent of animals run over in the winter/spring period (most rodenticides are applied in winter) carried detectable traces; if we accept that this sample excludes the unknown proportion of animals that had already died from poisoning (dead polecats don't often cross roads!), then it is very likely that more than half the population across England and Wales is exposed to rodenticides each year. Also, because analytical techniques are now more sensitive than during the 1990s, we can be pretty sure that the results of that study underestimated the extent of exposure in the polecat population.

Traps

Setting traps deliberately to catch or kill polecats is now illegal without a licence, but polecats remain vulnerable to accidental capture because their passion for investigating tunnels leads them into the covered places where lethal spring traps must, by law, be set. The legal use of spring traps is controlled by a series of Statutory Instruments called 'Spring Trap Approval Orders', which, amongst other considerations, seek to minimise impacts upon non-target species such as polecats: for example, one of the conditions is: 'So far as is practicable without unreasonably compromising its use for killing or taking target species, the trap must be used in a manner that minimises the likelihood of its killing, taking or injuring non-target species'. But can this laudable aim be achieved without specific guidance and mandatory exclusion measures? Furthermore some of the target pest species listed are much the same size as polecats so, for example, a spring trap set on the ground to kill rabbits, mink or grey squirrels will inevitably pose a risk to polecats. It follows that many spring traps are deployed in ways that make it inevitable that polecats are sometimes killed or injured.

It is difficult to estimate the numbers of polecats injured or killed by spring-trapping because trappers are unlikely to divulge such occurrences because of concerns about legal consequences. However, the recent VWT polecat surveys have revealed enough examples of polecats injured or killed in traps to suggest that this is the tip of a much larger iceberg. A particular problem arises where polecats encounter spring traps that are not designed to kill such a large animal, so the victim is held alive until it either dies or is dealt with by the trapper; by law all traps should be checked every day so that any suffering can be brought to a swift end, but are they? Regrettably I hear too many reports of spring traps left unchecked with trapped animals enduring slow and painful deaths. Even if such trapping has no significant impact upon the polecat's local conservation status, on welfare grounds alone there is a strong case for amending current practice to allow only those methods that do not harm non-target species. That's the challenge now facing trapping practitioners and the bodies that represent them; and if they fail to meet it then it is down to the legislators to clean up the act.

Polecats also enter cage traps set for mink, for example, even including those set on floating 'mink rafts' as part of wide-scale mink control operations. Provided that all traps are checked first thing every morning, and that trappers can readily identify polecats and release them as swiftly as possible, there should be little harm arising from such accidental captures (but see the caveats in the section on live-trapping on page 130).

STUDYING POLECATS

Field signs – a matter of scats and tracks

Field signs such as footprints and droppings are important to mammalogists because many of our study animals are difficult to observe, so identifying the signs they leave may be our best way of confirming the presence of a mammal at a particular location as part of a field survey. However, field signs can only be relied upon for this purpose if they are both easily detectable and distinctive; the polecat is awkward because its footprints and droppings (called scats) are identical to those of feral ferrets and difficult to separate from those of the American mink; worse still, polecats do not help us by depositing their scats in accessible and predictable places in the way that mink, otters and pine martens do, for example. Even when I was radio-tracking polecats and re-tracing their night-time movements the following day I found remarkably few scats; in keeping with others I concluded that polecats deposit most of their scats at their resting sites rather than out and about in their home ranges.

Polecat scats conform to the standard smallish mustelid pattern of a dark, smelly, twisty cigarette-sized excretion. In his charming Whittet book *Mammal Detective* the late Rob Strachan, supreme master of mammal surveying and possessor of a fine nose for distinguishing carnivore

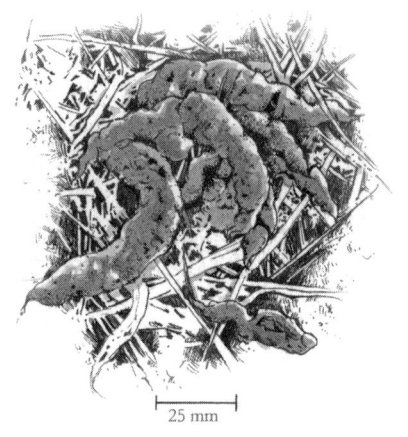

Polecats deposit most of their faeces, called scats, within or close to their den sites, where substantial piles may accumulate among the bedding.

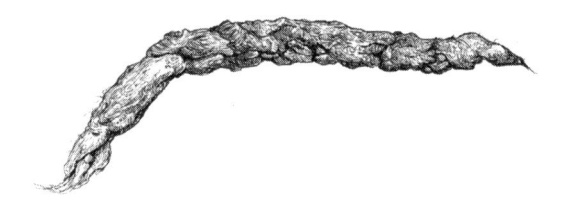

Polecat scats vary in size, shape, odour and colour according to variations in diet; this 'typical' scat is from a polecat that fed on rabbit; it is full of twisted fur and is about 8 mm wide and 70 mm long; mink scats may look identical!

scats, describes the scent of polecat scats as 'foul: foetid meat, distinctly unpleasant'; and mink scats emerge with a near-identical pedigree, viz 'foul: burnt rubber, rotten meat, unpleasant'. Even though mink are more closely associated with wetland habitats in Britain than polecats are it is unwise to assume that a scat found close to water is from a mink because polecats don't mind getting their feet wet in pursuit of a good meal; and scat contents are no help as a distinguishing feature because both mink and polecats consume a broad range of similar prey such as birds, mammals, amphibians and fish. So unless you have a miniature genetics lab in your back pocket (DNA analysis can readily separate the scats of mink from polecats), polecat and mink scats are essentially indistinguishable in appearance and smell. This fact, together with the feral ferret complication, means that the only certain way to identify a polecat scat is to view it emerging from the animal's bottom!

In ever-milder and mostly snow-free Britain it is not easy to find possible polecat footprints; we have to pin our hopes on chance encounters in muddy farmyards or on field edges, where we are lucky to find more than a few good individual prints. I cast envious eyes towards naturalist friends in colder countries, where extensive, long-lasting blankets of snow provide great opportunities to detect polecat prints, follow tracks and interpret their patterns to learn about polecat movements and behaviour. However, one January I was lucky to find a clear set of probable polecat footprints in fresh, shallow snow over 30 metres along a path near my home on the Malvern Hills. The tracks showed the animal's typical bounding gait, with both fore and hind feet landing close together in well-spaced clumps of four prints.

The arrangement of the prints in each clump depends upon the animal's speed of travel: in my case the polecat was bounding quite fast, with the hind feet landing just in front of and more widely spaced than the forefeet (at lower speeds the hind feet land beside, on top of, or behind the forefeet prints), with about 60 centimetres between the front of one clump of prints and the front of the next. Because of my Malvern polecat's speed, with most of the power provided by the hind feet pressing deep into the snow, the hind prints mostly showed all five toes and appeared broader (about 3 centimetres across) and clearer than the forefeet prints, which were less splayed and mostly showed only four of the five toes. In all prints the sharp claws had sliced through the snow at the front edge of each pad, giving each toe print a narrow teardrop shape.

Can we separate polecat and mink footprints?

Polecat footprints can be separated easily from those of smaller terrestrial mustelids such as stoats and weasels on the basis of their larger size. However, the footprints left by polecats and ferrets are identical, so cannot be separated at all; and those of mink present some challenges

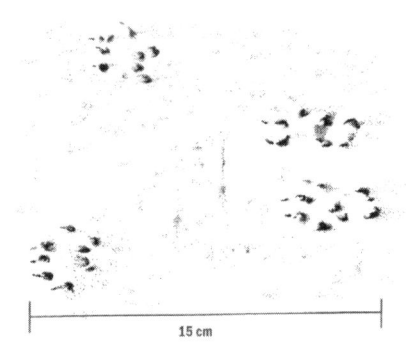

When bounding fast a polecat's hind feet tend to land just ahead of its forefeet; and because the forefeet provide less power their prints are usually narrower and typically don't show all five toes.

Polecat tracks in snow on The Malvern Hills, Worcestershire, showing the typical mustelid bounding pattern with all four feet landing close together.

because they are very similar in size and shape to those of polecats and ferrets. Nevertheless it is important to distinguish the footprints of polecats/ferrets and American mink if we can, not least because polecats sometimes enter and leave their footprints in the floating 'mink rafts' developed by the Game and Wildlife Conservation Trust (GWCT) and now widely used for monitoring and trapping as part of mink control operations along Britain's waterways; also, structured or informal field surveys for mink have traditionally been based on assumptions that their footprints are easily identified in mud along the water's edge or under bridges, so we need to ensure that such surveys are not undermined by mistaken identities now that the polecat has become widespread in Britain once more.

The underside of a polecat's left forefoot (left) and left hind foot (right); redrawn from photographs by John Martin.

Polecats and American mink have the same basic footprint design on both their fore and hind feet: this consists of five smallish toe pads arranged around and in front of lobed interdigital pads that are normally merged into a single arc; very often one of the outer toe pads does not show up in footprints unless they are made in soft and yielding mud or snow; claw marks usually show up in front of the toe pads in soft mud, in which case they tend to be connected with the toe prints giving them a slim, tear-drop shape; but in firm mud the claw marks are often not visible; in very soft mud the mesial webbing (flaps of skin between the toes) may show up in prints of both species. One difference between the fore and hind prints is that occasionally a small, round proximal (heel) pad shows up just behind the interdigital pads in the forefoot prints of both species.

The footprints of polecats and American mink are very similar in size, with the adult males of both species having larger prints than those of adult females (of course when juveniles are present in summer there is a size overlap between the prints of adult females and young males). Bearing in mind the gender sizes differences, differences in size and shape between the fore and hind feet, and variations arising due to patterns of locomotion, the footprints of both species recorded in high quality mud or snow typically fall within the range 30–45 millimetres long (excluding claw marks) by 25–40 millimetres wide (however, on the Malvern Hills I did once find presumed polecat prints in firm mud that were 49 millimetres long and 46 millimetres wide, so these must have been made by a particularly large male). There is a tendency for mink footprints to have their toes more widely splayed than those of polecats, which by contrast have more forward-pointing toes, but how reliable is this as a distinguishing feature?

With much overlap in size and shape, how an earth can we use footprints to separate the two species? The Belarusian mustelid fieldworker Vadim Sidorovich has described some qualitative differences between American mink and polecat footprints: he found that although a footprint of each species may cover the same total area, because the polecat has larger toe pads and interdigital pads than does the mink, these pads occupy a visibly greater proportion of the whole print area; secondly, the claw marks in polecat footprints appear more crooked or curved than the mink's, which are shorter and straighter; finally, Sidorovich noted that when the animals are bounding through snow there are differences in the clumping of footprints, with polecats tending to have a more even mix (40–60 per cent) over a 300-metre run of clumps of four and two prints (because of complete registering of hind prints on fore prints in the latter case), whereas the American mink has one or other clumping pattern dominating to the tune of 80 per cent over a 300-metre run; also the American mink prints tend to be clumped at a slant in relation to the direction of travel, while the polecat print clumps were more perpendicular to the direction of travel. (These last two features depend upon the availability of rather more snow than we usually find in Britain these days!)

During her study of American mink and polecats in the Thames Valley near Oxford, Lauren Harrington applied some neat science in order to detect and quantify any differences in footprints of the two species. Using freshly live-trapped wild animals, which she released into a special wooden box containing the same moist clay as is used in the GWCT mink rafts, she photographed a large sample of clear 'walking only' footprints of adult polecats and American mink of both genders alongside a ruler to aid subsequent measurements. Lauren then took a host of careful measurements and used multivariate analyses to develop an algorithm (scientist-speak for a cunning and complicated formula) capable of distinguishing footprints of the two species, regardless of gender and which foot was involved (left, right, fore or hind).

Before developing her algorithm, Lauren Harrington first considered whether a single feature could be used to separate the species' footprints: although male mink footprints were significantly wider than those of polecats of both sexes and those of female mink, there was too much overlap between species for width to be a reliable distinguishing feature on its own; then, testing one of Sidorovich's observations, Harrington found that although crooked claw marks were more often found in polecat footprints (37 per cent compared with just 3 per cent in mink prints), the fact that the majority of polecat prints had straight claw marks just like those in mink prints also ruled this out as a distinguishing feature (though any footprint with crooked claw marks is much more likely to have been made by a polecat); claw length also had some value in footprints, because polecats generally had longer claws so that any print having a distance greater than 6 millimetres from the top of the claw mark to the top of the toe pad would be a polecat, but measurements of less than 6 millimetres could be from either species; finally, because the toes in mink footprints tend to be more splayed than those of polecats, any print with a distance of more than 4 millimetres between the pads of toes 2 and 3 would be a mink, but any less than 4 millimetres could be from either species. So, despite some promising differences among these individual features, none was sufficiently reliable to serve on its own as a means to separate the footprints of polecats and American mink.

Harrington next chose six specific footprint measurements that all differed significantly between the two species in order to produce a

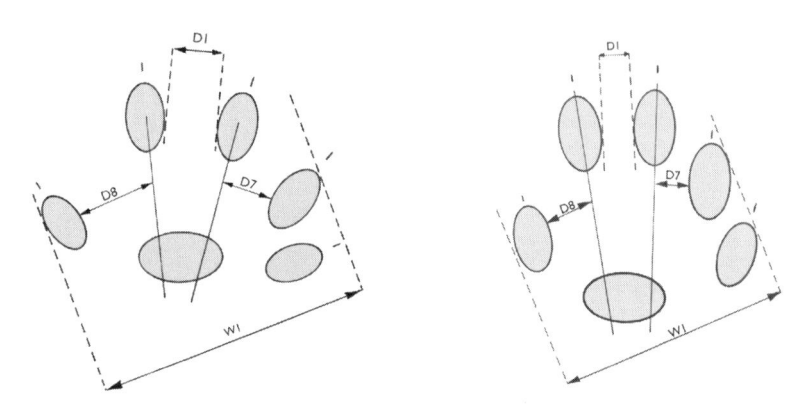

Schematic footprints of mink (left) and polecat (right), showing the four measurements developed by Lauren Harrington to separate the species under perfect conditions (redrawn with kind permission of Lauren Harrington).

discriminant function model that correctly classified 98.6 per cent of footprints. However, a simpler model based on just three measurements correctly classified 97.3 per cent of footprints using the following formula (based on the measurements shown in the schematic footprint drawing above):

If 1.7 − 0.75(W1) + 2.43(D1) + 1.85(mean D7, D8) > 0, classify the footprint as mink, if < 0 classify the footprint as polecat.

There is a health warning, however: Harrington points out that all her measurements were made of clearly defined footprints on well-maintained tracking plates covered with very smooth clay; the variable quality of footprints found in more natural situations may not provide the accurate measurements required for the formula to work reliably, but it is certainly worth a try! Good quality callipers are essential if measurements are to be taken in the field.

Camera-trapping
One of the best ways to view and learn about your local polecats, especially if you have neither the time nor inclination for a labour-intensive (for you)

and potentially intrusive (for the polecats) study based on live-trapping (which in any case requires a licence), is to use a 'camera trap' to record night-time action while you sleep. These devices use motion- or heat-sensitive detectors that trigger a camera to record still or moving digital images, with each file labelled with date and time; at night they use infrared light to illuminate the image so as not to frighten the subject; they were first developed to help lazy North American hunters to determine when and where they should sit to maximise their chances of shooting their favoured quarry. Now much more affordable and reliable than they once were, camera traps are widely used by naturalists and researchers as a cost-effective means of detecting and learning about nocturnal carnivores and other elusive animals.

Because polecats live at low population densities and do not make distinctive paths or runs that we can readily detect, the best way to 'catch' them on a camera trap is to use bait to attract them to a suitable location where you can set up a camera with a low risk of interference or theft; this could even be your garden if you live in an area where polecats are present. Knowing that polecats prefer to stay close to good cover I normally choose an overgrown hedge or woodland edge where I tie a fresh road-killed rabbit to something solid so that it cannot be removed by a polecat or other animals; the bait should be under cover so that it is out of view of buzzards and crows; and it is important to avoid placing bait close to a run used by foxes or badgers, otherwise they will fill your camera with shots of 'non-target' animals. Non-target photos are an inevitable part of wildlife camera-trapping, but I quite enjoy the fun of searching through dozens of photos of cats, wood mice and foxes; and it makes it all the more exciting when you finally encounter your target animal.

With some strikingly marked wild animals, such as tigers, camera traps can be used to census populations based on individual differences in fur colour patterns. This may not be possible with polecats because most animals look much the same, but some individuals that visit a camera trap might be separated on the basis of slight differences in size and in the pattern of facial markings, for example. Many people have successfully photographed polecats on camera traps, including in gardens where the animals readily come to take bait.

One constraint to bear in mind is that most camera traps use infrared light to illuminate subjects at night and this produces greyish images that make it difficult to distinguish between a true polecat and a ferrety specimen. However, if a polecat can be persuaded (by provision of tasty titbits, for example) to visit a site frequently to take its own photos, it will soon learn to tolerate a bright flash so that full colour images can be taken.

Live-trapping

Polecats are not difficult animals to trap, which is partly why they were so easily exterminated from most of Britain around the end of the nineteenth century. Their keen interest in investigating any hole or burrow, especially if it smells of something tasty, means that mammalogists can set and bait cage traps in ways that make captures quite likely if polecats are present. As their name suggests, cage traps are made of strong wire mesh such as weldmesh; they usually function by means of a treadle close to the rear end that, when depressed, releases a sprung door to trap the animal. Cage traps come in different sizes depending upon the target species, from foxes down through rabbits, mink and squirrels to rats, and polecats have been accidentally caught in most of these. Most studies of polecats have used cage traps designed for mink, because both animals are similar in size.

There are important issues to consider before making any decision to start a live-trapping study of polecats: firstly, there are legal restrictions on the killing or taking of polecats, so any intentional trapping of a polecat requires a licence from the appropriate government agency, and a licence may not be granted unless good reasons are given to justify a trapping study; secondly, trapping can be stressful and inevitably interferes with the movements of any trapped animal, with the risk of adverse impacts on welfare if, for example, a hungry polecat is prevented from feeding or a lactating female is separated from her young kits for several hours.

So trapping of polecats should not be embarked upon without a great deal of careful thought; and it is always important to ask the question, 'Can I possibly gather the same information in a less intrusive way?' Fortunately, there have been several recent advances in 'non-invasive' methods of studying mammals, such as camera-trapping and DNA analysis of scats and hair samples, which means that live-trapping is no longer the crucial source of information that it once was. Nevertheless, live-trapping is still justifiable if a study necessitates a researcher handling a live wild polecat, for example to fit or remove a radio collar, or to take a blood sample.

Through my work with The Vincent Wildlife Trust I learnt that, when it is essential, live-trapping of polecats can be done in ways that minimise stress and the risk of harm to study animals and any non-target captures. So, having reached the decision that live-trapping is truly necessary, it is important to follow the best possible method. A crucial welfare measure is the provision of abundant dry hay (not straw) on top of the trap and beneath any local materials used to camouflage the trap site. This hay achieves two functions: it provides a soft and yielding material for a trapped polecat to pull at with its teeth, thereby avoiding the risk of damage to its teeth and gums that can arise if it attacks the wire mesh; and because a trapped polecat tends to pull lots of the hay inside the trap it creates a mass of insulating material in which the animal can hide and gain protection from wind, rain or low temperatures.

The Chartered Institute of Ecology and Environmental Management (CIEEM) has produced a technical guidance note, *Competencies for Species Survey: Polecat*, that sets out the knowledge, skills and experience required for professional survey work on polecats.

Hair tubes and footprint tunnels

Among the non-invasive approaches to studying scarce mammals are specially designed tubes or tunnels supplied with devices that collect a few hairs or footprints of any animal passing through them. Hairs can be scrutinised under high-powered microscopes or subject to DNA analysis to determine species, and footprints can be compared with sample sets for the same purpose. Whilst polecats willingly pass through such devices and leave hairs and footprints, these cannot reliably be separated from those of feral ferrets for the reasons explained above. Further information on using these methods can be obtained from bodies like The Mammal Society and The Vincent Wildlife Trust.

Watching polecats

Ever since I first became involved with the species in the early 1990s I have often been asked (usually by desperate wildlife film-makers) where is the best place to go to watch wild polecats. As I get older my answers get progressively shorter and less polite, for there is no easy fix: polecats are not like badgers with their distinctive main setts and 'set your watch by it' emergence times; they are elusive, unpredictable and mainly nocturnal, so are almost impossible to watch at our convenience. Apart from when I was live-trapping or radio-tracking them, all my sightings of wild polecats were very occasional, brief and entirely down to chance, and most were seen on the roads at night in my car headlights. Only if you are fortunate enough to find a breeding female with kits at a den are you likely to experience the rare thrill of watching polecats other than by chance, until she moves them to another den; but make sure you don't add to her stress!

POLECATS AND THE LAW

It is typical of our poor historical treatment of the humble polecat that, having blitzed it from most of Britain, we then failed to give it full legal protection in the early decades of its recovery: for the polecat initially received only partial protection through its listing on Schedule 6 of the Wildlife and Countryside Act 1981, which limits the ways in which polecats may be killed or taken. So one may shoot a polecat with an appropriate weapon, but intentional trapping of a polecat is illegal without a licence. Is this an example of the fickle favouritism that guides the way we distribute our legal largesse? Had the polecat been a bat, a bird or a badger (perhaps it should have changed its name to bolecat?!), you can bet we would have smothered it with sufficient statutory protection to paper a small office.

There have been some changes to the mechanism (but not the level) of the polecat's protection in Britain since the 1981 Act, notably in Scotland where different legislation is now in place, but the limited cover is essentially the same. Protection against cruel ill-treatment in captivity (for example when a wild polecat is held in a trap) is provided under the Wild Mammals (Protection) Act 1996, and in England and Wales the polecat also gets a mention under the Natural Environment and Rural Communities Act 2006, which requires all public bodies to have regard for biodiversity conservation. Interpreting legislation relating to polecats is not easy because it has not been fully tested in court. My understanding is that anyone using potentially harmful traps must take reasonable precautions to avoid killing or injuring a polecat, although in my experience many trappers believe that accidental captures in such traps are not illegal. The Game and Wildlife Conservation Trust has developed an exclusion device to prevent polecats entering 'tunnel traps', so the means exists for those willing to use it (but very few actually do so because the device excludes some of the animals they wish to kill). Despite this useful advance, most tunnel-trapping in Britain remains woefully non-specific so is likely to cause death or injury to polecats and other non-target species.

Please don't rely on this lay interpretation of the law and licensing relating to polecats. For a definitive opinion it is best to consult an environmental lawyer or seek advice from the relevant statutory agencies: currently Scottish Natural Heritage, Natural Resources Wales and Natural England.

FURTHER READING

Apart from VWT survey reports and dry scientific papers, there has been remarkably little written about polecats and almost nothing that might appeal to the general public. One exception is Paddy Sleeman's Stoats and Weasels, Polecats and Pine Martens published by Whittet Books in 1989. Because it covered four species in one small book it could not explore the polecat in any depth, and in any case it preceded most of the recent studies of polecats in Britain.

Birks, J. D. S. (2008) *The Polecat Survey of Britain 2004–2006: A Report on the Polecat's Distribution, Status and Conservation* (The Vincent Wildlife Trust, Ledbury)

Birks, J. D. S. and Kitchener, A. C. (1999) *The Distribution and Status of the Polecat Mustela Putorius in Britain in the 1990*s (The Vincent Wildlife Trust, London)

Chartered Institute of Ecology and Environmental Management (2013), *Competencies for Species Survey: Polecat* (CIEEM Technical Guidance Series, www.cieem.net)

Cresswell, W. J., Birks, J. D. S., Dean, M., Pacheco, M., Trewhella, W. J., Wells, D. and Wray, S. (eds.) (2012) *UK BAP Mammals: Interim Guidance for Survey Methodologies, Impact Assessment and Mitigation* (The Mammal Society, Southampton)

Langley, P. J. W and Yalden, D. W. (1977) *'The decline of the rarer carnivores in Great Britain during the nineteenth century'*, Mammal Review, 7, 95–116

Lovegrove, R. (2007) *Silent Fields: The Long Decline of a Nation's Wildlife* (Oxford University Press)

McKay, J. (2002) *The Complete Guide to Ferrets* (Swanhill Press, Shrewsbury)

McKay, J. (2006) *Ferret Breeding: A Modern Scientific Approach* (Swanhill Press, Shrewsbury)

Tapper, S. (1992) *Game Heritage: An Ecological Review from Shooting and Gamekeeping Records* (Game Conservancy Ltd, Fordingbridge)

The Vincent Wildlife Trust (2014) *Polecats and Ferrets: How to Tell Them Apart* (The Vincent Wildlife Trust, Ledbury)

SOURCES OF INFORMATION

There are very few organisations that stand up for the polecat in Britain, so this list is rather short:

The Vincent Wildlife Trust organises conservation-directed research on polecats and conducts distribution surveys.
The VWT, 3 & 4 Bronsil Courtyard, Eastnor, Ledbury, Herefordshire HR8 1EP
www.vwt.org.uk

The Mammal Society brings people together who are interested in studying and conserving wild mammals.
www.mammal.org.uk

If you find an injured or orphaned polecat, it is best to contact the **RSPCA** so that it can be released back into the wild once fit enough.
www.rspca.org.uk

INDEX

activity patterns 67–8, 70, 99, 105
albino 12, 18, 48, 56–7
alopecia 113–14
amphibians 67, 79–83, 85, 87–93, 95–6, 101, 105, 109, 115
aposematic (colouration) 6

baculum 52
badger 5–6, 11, 64, 79, 113, 117, 129, 132–3
'bandit mask' 6–8, 16, 27, 52–3, 56, 75
birds 27, 31–2, 34, 37, 78–82, 85–91, 99, 101, 105, 109, 123, 133
birth 68, 73–4, 78, 99
black–footed ferret 7–8, 10
body
　length 6, 50–1
　shape 5, 48–50
　weight 6, 49–51, 67–8, 70, 72
bounty payments 26
bovine TB 113

camera–trapping 128–30
carrion 80, 88–9, 115
CIEEM (Competencies for Species Survey: Polecat) 131
communication 65–7
competition 13, 23, 36, 44–5, 47, 62, 86, 88, 94–5, 97, 106–9
　scent 6, 58, 64–6, 110
　vocal 66–7

defensive stink 6, 24, 27, 65, 99, 110–11, 115
dens 68, 74, 76, 79–80, 99, 102–5
　natal 67–8, 72–6
dentition 51, 106
diet 79–95, 98, 105, 109, 123
　gender variations 84–6
　regional variations 88–93
　seasonal variations 85
diseases 36, 47, 78, 94–5, 112–13
dispersal 55, 61, 68, 77–8, 104, 118
DNA 19–20, 123, 130–1
domestication 13–18, 22–3, 51

erythristic ('red' polecat) 48, 56
European polecat distribution 6

families (polecat) 68, 76, 116–17
farmyard 27, 64–5, 67–8, 73, 78, 86–7, 97–8, 104–5, 113, 119, 123
ferret (domestic and feral) 9, 11–23, 41–2, 44, 48, 51–2, 54–7, 66, 71, 75, 79, 101, 112–14, 122–4, 130–1
ferreting 12–13, 18, 52
field signs 122–8
　footprints 123–8
　scats 79, 122–3
fighting 50, 57, 67, 68–70, 72, 117
fish 82, 88–9, 109, 123
fisher 93
fitch 12, 24, 26
footprint tunnel 131
foraging 58, 67–8, 73–4, 76, 79–96, 98–9, 102, 104–6, 115, 117, 119
fossil record 9, 25
foxes 26, 34, 36, 64, 79, 101, 110–11, 113, 117, 129–30
frogs 58, 80, 83, 85, 88–9, 92, 98, 101
fur
　colour 6, 12, 18–19, 22, 48, 52–7
　seasonal variations 48, 50, 53–4, 114
　structure 53
　trade 26

Game and Wildlife Conservation Trust 125, 127, 133
game shooting 4, 27, 31–4, 37
gamekeepers 21, 26, 31–2, 34–7, 50
genetics 9–10, 13–14, 18–22, 48, 51, 55–6, 78
genotype 20–1
gestation 73–4
gin trap 28, 31, 37

habitat 6, 13, 32, 39, 45, 47, 60, 63, 73, 79, 93–101
　microhabitat 98–9
　preferences 97–8
　seasonal variations in use 97

hair tube 131
Hansard 25, 29
hearing 58
hybridisation 8–10, 13, 19–21, 55
home range (and territory) 6, 60–2, 64–5, 74–8, 96, 102, 104, 108–9, 122
hunting (of polecats with hounds) 26
hybridisation 8–10, 13, 20–1, 48, 55

IUCN listing 8, 47

kits 18, 48, 50, 69, 71–6, 99, 117, 130, 132

lactation 68, 74–6, 130
legal protection 13, 19, 133
lifespan 76
litter size 74

Mammal Society 131, 136
marbled polecat 8
mating 6, 20, 50, 55, 57, 64, 67, 69–74, 107, 117
mating scars 57, 68, 72
mink 11, 57, 73, 112, 121, 123–4, 130
  American 5, 10–11, 47, 49, 53–4, 72, 79, 92, 94–5, 97, 106–9, 122, 125–8
  European 10, 92, 107–8
moult 68, 73, 114
mortality 44–5, 74, 77–8, 96, 115–21
Mustela robusta 10
Mustela stromeri 8
Myxomatosis 36, 41, 79–80, 82, 90, 95

names (historical and foreign, of polecat) 24–6
National Museums Scotland 19, 80, 85
newts 80, 88
North Africa (polecat status) 9

oestrus 69–71, 73
otter 5–6, 11, 34, 64, 79, 88, 92–3, 95, 106, 108, 122
ovulation 69–71

parasites 76, 112
pelage character total (PCT) scoring 54–5

persecution 3, 13, 26–8, 31–5, 37, 42
phenotype 19–22, 55
pine marten 5, 24, 32, 34, 88, 110–1, 122
play 67, 75, 117
polecat–ferret 9, 11, 19, 22, 40–3, 53
population 20–1, 27, 42–5, 48, 54–6, 63–4, 69, 78, 95–6, 107, 109, 113, 118, 120
  decline 21, 26–7, 31–6, 45, 47, 94–5
  density 60–3, 70, 96, 113, 129
  distribution (in Britain) 39–46
  estimate (Mesolithic, Britain) 63
  estimate (recent, Britain) 62–3
  recovery 3, 14, 21, 36–47, 62–3, 95, 108, 133
post–orbital constriction 14–15, 51–2
poultry 4, 24, 27, 81, 101
predators (of polecats) 6, 8, 53, 73, 99, 110–11, 115
pregnancy 69–73
prey–switching 88–9

rabbits 12–14, 16–18, 24, 35–6, 41–2, 47, 52, 58, 60, 62–3, 74–6, 79–91, 93–6, 98, 101, 103–5, 109, 115, 117, 121, 123, 129–30
rabbit–trapping 35–6
radio–tracking 27, 44, 58, 64, 73, 79–80, 83–6, 97–9, 103–5, 122, 132
RSPCA 44, 76, 136
rats 12, 27, 63, 67, 85–7, 97–8, 105, 119, 130
reintroductions (of polecats) 20, 40–6, 61
reputation 24–9
road casualties 19, 22, 38–9, 48, 57, 67–72, 74, 76–7, 80, 112, 115, 118, 120
rodenticides 78, 115, 119–20
rodents 7–8, 27, 68, 85–92, 96, 98, 101, 105, 119

Saharan striped polecat 8
scats 64, 66
  analysis 79–81, 85–6
  size and shape 122–3
  smell 123
scavenging 101, 117

137

scent glands 6, 27, 65
scent marking 64, 66
sexual dimorphism 6, 49–51, 85–6
Shakespeare 25
skeleton 51–2
skull 10, 14–15, 51–2
steppe polecat 6–8, 10, 14, 15
stoat 5–6, 36, 48, 72–3, 106, 111–12, 124
suburban polecats 96–101

toads 80, 83, 85, 88–9, 92–3, 98
territoriality 6, 44, 64–5, 68, 71, 77, 102
trapping (polecats) 11, 22, 31–2, 36–7, 41, 44, 48, 61–2, 121, 130–3
  camera trapping 128–30
  licence (for trapping polecats) 11, 48, 61, 120, 129–30, 133

tunnel or spring traps 37, 115, 120–1, 133

Vincent Wildlife Trust (VWT) 11, 20, 22, 27, 39–41, 45, 48, 50, 54–7, 60–2, 71, 74, 76, 83–6, 88, 97, 99, 103–5, 111, 117–21, 136

watching polecats 131–2
water vole 80, 89, 95
weaning 74–6
weasel 5–6, 48, 112, 124
  Japanese 10
  Siberian (or kolinsky) 10
wetlands 47, 85, 94–8, 109, 123
WildCRU 108

zorilla (striped or African polecat) 8